The Lobster

A24

	FOREWORD Written by Emma Stone	6
I	**THE LOBSTER** Written by Yorgos Lanthimos and Efthimis Filippou	10
II	**24 FRAMES**	88
III	**BLINDED BY LOVE** Written by Ottessa Moshfegh	142
IV	**ON SET** Photos by Yorgos Lanthimos	152

5

what you are about to read
is
about people who must share a trait,
find a mate
or they will be turned
into an animal
of their choosing
from the animals they already are.

there is very little
that can make you laugh and
retch all at once.

he is handcuffed to his belt and
has all matching clothes
she comes in and sits and tells him
not to let it get him down
for these are the rules
surreal, and funny.

and when her body lies contorted on the ground
from a suicide attempt because
she's desperate
and lonely and she's never going to find
the love she needs to live (this is literal)
we are sick and it is funny.

when she kicks the dog to death
to prove
she doesn't care at all
she is heartless and wants to test him, see if he's
up to snuff
it is grotesque
and it is funny.

when he bangs his head on the table
over and over to break his nose
to watch it bleed and be like her
so he can find hope, and she, companionship
you know what i am saying.

once in a while
somebody comes along
that sees things as they are,
surreal and sick and grotesque and
funny.
i am glad he does. they do.

they have a vantage
(yorgos and efthimis - i am talking about the writers)
and he the eyes
(yorgos - he is also the director)
that have changed the way i see
and understand
and that's not just me or else
you wouldn't be here
reading this.
isn't it surreal?
isn't it funny?
isn't it true?

when i speak broken greek
or write a poem
or laugh at something that should break my heart
or cry at a commercial
to try to share a trait
to meet in the middle
to not become an animal
i feel more animal than ever
and maybe sometimes
that's better.

and then there's the horse with the beautiful hair.
just funny.

this is "the lobster."

EMMA STONE

SECTION

10

I

SECTION I

THE LOBSTER

Written by Yorgos Lanthimos and Efthimis Filippou

EXT. COUNTRY ROAD - DAY

A WOMAN drives. She is on a country road, with fields on either side. She reaches a deserted spot where three donkeys stand on the right side of the road. The woman pulls over, puts on a pair of gloves, gets out of the car, checks to see if there is anyone nearby or if she is being watched, runs towards the donkeys, shoots one of them many times over, runs back to the car and drives away.

OPENING CREDITS

I. THE TOWN

INT. CITY APARTMENT SITTING ROOM - MORNING

A man around 45 years old, DAVID, sits on a sofa. DAVID'S WIFE, around 40 years old, stands and leans against a bookcase. David is shortsighted and wears glasses. His wife also wears glasses. Next to David lies a DOG. David is crying. The woman is not.

> DAVID'S WIFE
> I'm really sorry.
>
> (pause)
>
> DAVID
> Does he wear glasses or contact lenses?
>
> DAVID'S WIFE
> Glasses.
>
> (pause)

David doesn't look at her. He stares at the floor. He swivels a glass of grapefruit juice on the table with his hand. David's wife seems sad. She looks at her watch a couple of times. She hesitates, but finally talks.

> DAVID'S WIFE (CONT'D)
> You'll have to hurry up. They'll be here quite soon.

David leaves the room. As he goes to the bedroom, his wife keeps talking to him.

> DAVID'S WIFE (CONT'D)
> Don't worry. I'm sure you'll find the right woman really soon. A woman of average shortsightedness, just like you.

INT. CITY APARTMENT BEDROOM - MORNING

David picks out clothes from the wardrobe and gets dressed. His movements are slow and unhurried, as if he doesn't want these final preparations to end. He stares at his slippers next to the bed. He decides not to take them with him.

> FEMALE V.O.
> He decided that his brown leather shoes were the best pair to wear. He went through the corridor into the sitting room. There he saw the other man for the first and last time. He was very handsome.

INT. CITY APARTMENT SITTING ROOM - MORNING

David goes to the sitting room. In the sitting room sits a MAN. He too is shortsighted and wears glasses. He eats a tuna-mayonnaise sandwich.

> FEMALE V.O.
> He was eating a tuna-mayonnaise sandwich and wearing a pair of black lace-up shoes. She was in the kitchen. David sat in the armchair and looked at his watch. His wife entered the room and left a glass of Diet Coke for the man eating the sandwich.

INT. CITY APARTMENT SITTING ROOM - MORNING

David sits in the armchair. The two men do not look at or talk to each other. David's wife enters, holding a glass of Diet Coke with ice and a slice of lemon. She leaves the glass in front of the man eating the sandwich. She looks at her watch and then out the window. Everyone waits in silence. They all avoid making eye contact. David grabs a coffee table book from the coffee table next to him. He flicks through the pages quickly, look-ing at the pictures without any real interest. He just goes through the motions. The dog sits next to him.

> FEMALE V.O.
> David picked up a book called "The Most Famous Lighthouses in the World" and pretended to read. He was thinking his wife didn't love him at all anymore. He didn't burst into tears and he didn't think that the first thing most people do when they realise someone doesn't love them anymore is cry.

The doorbell rings. The woman gets up and answers the door. Two men dressed as WAITERS enter.

> 70-YEAR-OLD WAITER
> Good afternoon.

> DAVID'S WIFE
> Good afternoon.

> 70-YEAR-OLD WAITER
> Which of these two gentlemen is the one you're breaking up with?

> DAVID'S WIFE
> Not the man eating the sandwich. The man with the brown shoes.

David gets up. His wife goes over to him. He closes the book and leaves it on the table.

> DAVID'S WIFE (CONT'D)
> You can take the book with you, if you like.

> DAVID
> No, that's okay.

He buttons up his jacket and fixes his hair with his hands.

                    DAVID'S WIFE
          Are you ready? Did you pack that pain
          relief cream for your back?

                    DAVID
          Yes.

                    DAVID'S WIFE
          You're healthy, you have many interests,
          you have good taste. Everything will be
          fine.

David looks at the waiters.

                    DAVID
          I'm ready.

EXT. CITY ROAD - MORNING

The waiters lead David to a coach. The dog follows them
and gets into the vehicle with David.

EXT. HOTEL COACH - MORNING

There are another four people sitting in the coach: two
WOMEN, a BALD MAN and a MAN whom we will call "Limping
Man." They all sit in different parts of the coach. David
takes a window seat. The waiters sit together behind
the WAITER-DRIVER. One of the two women gets up from her
seat and goes over to where David sits. She looks at the
dog and smiles at him but does not stroke him. She looks
a little afraid of him. She strokes the dog above his
hind legs, as far from the animal's mouth as possible.

                    BISCUIT WOMAN
          Your dog is so beautiful. What's his name?

                    DAVID
          Bob.

                    BISCUIT WOMAN
          Hello, Bob. I'm Anna. I love dogs so much.
          I'm sure Bob senses this and knows that
          we're going to get along famously. I've
          heard the journey takes over an hour. I've
          got butter biscuits and hazelnuts in my
          bag. I can give you some if you're hungry.
          I mean, we can share them. I can give the
          dog some hazelnuts too, or a biscuit.

One of the waiters gets up from his seat and goes over
to the woman.

                    30-YEAR-OLD WAITER
          I'm afraid you'll have to return to your
          seat until we reach our destination.

                    BISCUIT WOMAN
          I see. How long will that be, roughly?

                    70-YEAR-OLD WAITER
          The journey lasts a little over an hour.

The woman goes back to her seat. She opens her bag and
eats a butter biscuit. She takes a quick look around at
the other people in the vehicle.

INT. HOTEL COACH - MORNING

David looks out the window. They have left the town and there are some woods beside the road. Suddenly a rock hits the window. David is a little shocked. He notices that the waiters do not react. David sees some people wearing ponchos running alongside the coach. They are shouting but we cannot hear what they are saying. More rocks strike the vehicle. The driver speeds up and gets away. He is completely unfazed by the incident.

EXT. HOTEL CARPARK - MORNING

The coach goes through the hotel gates and comes to a stop. The gates are opened by TWO WAITER-GUARDS, who wave to the driver. The waiters have automatic rifles slung across their backs. The hotel is a large building surrounded by a tall fence. It looks quite well-maintained and clean. The plants are in excellent condition and it is immediately clear that this is one of those large hotel complexes that can accommodate a large number of guests. At the entrance, the flags of various countries fly on tall poles. A number of people stand and watch from the room windows. One of them waves. Biscuit Woman, filled with optimism, waves back. The passengers get off the coach. The two waiters lead them to the entrance in a line. Limping Man is slow and falls behind because of his limp.

II. THE HOTEL NEAR THE CITY

INT. HOTEL RECEPTION - DAY

The hotel lobby is quiet. There are only a few people around apart from the RECEPTIONIST. On the walls are various classic-looking paintings, all of which show couples in a characteristic pose: the man seated in an armchair with the woman standing by his side. There are also some paintings, again in a classic style, of animals such as a horse, a duck or some other bird. The receptionist is a young woman with a friendly face and a calm voice. Biscuit Woman, the other woman, David, Limping Man, and the Bald Man stand in front of the reception desk.

                    RECEPTIONIST
          Welcome. Have any of you stayed in the
          hotel before?

                    BISCUIT WOMAN
          I have.

                    RECEPTIONIST
          Excellent. Then you know the rules. If you
          like, you can wait in the lobby. You'll
          find today's papers, and we can bring you
          tea or coffee or a soft drink.

                    BISCUIT WOMAN
          I'd like to hear the rules again, if you
          don't mind. I mean, it's been ten years
          since I was last here and I've forgotten a
          number of things. Like the bit with the
          days where you hunt the people in the woods
          with a bow and arrow, the night of the
          slaughter and so on.

> RECEPTIONIST
> Some things have changed. We use tranquilliser guns now instead of bows and arrows and the night of the slaughter has been done away with. I'll go over everything again with you. I don't mind at all.

> BISCUIT WOMAN
> Does Toby still work here?

> RECEPTIONIST
> Who's Toby?

> BISCUIT WOMAN
> Toby. The outdoor bar waiter.

> RECEPTIONIST
> I don't know. You'll have to ask one of the outdoor bar staff. I'd like you all to form a line. I suggest the gentlemen allow the ladies to go first, although this isn't compulsory. You can sort this out amongst yourselves.

The gentlemen allow the ladies to go first.

INT. HOTEL LOBBY - MORNING

David is the last to be served. He keeps hold of the Alsatian with one hand and rests his other hand on the reception desk. The dog seems anxious, and barks. David tries to calm it down but doesn't succeed. The dog barks throughout the exchange that follows. The receptionist is typing some information on a laptop. The computer is connected to a small camera. She takes a close up photo of David.

> RECEPTIONIST
> Well, sir, you said you've never been on your own before, correct?

> DAVID
> No, never.

The receptionist fills in a form.

> RECEPTIONIST
> Are you allergic to any foods?

> DAVID
> No.

> RECEPTIONIST
> Your last relationship lasted how many years?

> DAVID
> Around twelve.

> RECEPTIONIST
> Do you remember how long exactly?

David tries to calm and quiet the dog but fails.

> DAVID
> Eleven years and one month.

                    RECEPTIONIST
          Sexual preference?

                    DAVID
          Women.

David has second thoughts.

                    DAVID (CONT'D)
          However, I had one homosexual experience
          in the past, in college. Is there a bisexu-
          al option available?

                    RECEPTIONIST
          No sir, this option is no longer available
          since last summer, due to several opera-
          tional problems. I am afraid you have to
          decide right now if you want to be regis-
          tered as a homosexual or a heterosexual.

                    DAVID
          Then I think I should be registered as a
          heterosexual.

                    RECEPTIONIST
          Any children?

                    DAVID
          No.

                    RECEPTIONIST
          And the dog?

                    DAVID
          My brother. He was here a couple of years
          ago but he didn't make it. You might
          remember him. Medium build, 48 years old,
          bald patch, blond.

                    RECEPTIONIST
          I'm afraid not, sir. Okay, now I'd like you
          to write your name clearly on this form.

She hands him the form to fill in.

                    RECEPTIONIST (CONT'D)
          In capital letters. And sign it.

We see the golf course empty. On a tennis court we see a
MAN and a WOMAN playing.

                    RECEPTIONIST (V.O.) (CONT'D)
          You're not allowed to use the volleyball
          or tennis courts, these are only for the
          couples. You can use the facilities for in-
          dividual sports, such as squash and golf.

At the hotel bar, the BARMAN mixes a cocktail. Someone is
drinking a Campari alone (CAMPARI MAN).

                    RECEPTIONIST (V.O.) (CONT'D)
          You can stay in the hotel for up to 45
          days. You'll be staying in a single room.
          If everything goes well and you make it,
          you'll be moved to a double room. Every
          Saturday there's a dance in the main hall.
          You're in luck, because tomorrow's Satur-

>   day. Here's a leaflet with the hotel rules.
>   I'd like you to read it carefully and
>   if you have any questions, don't hesitate
>   to ask me for help.

In the hotel kitchen, WAITERS wash the dishes. They then lay out a buffet. One of the waiters has dirtied his shirt. Another sprays his shirt with stain-removal fluid, waits for it to dry and then wipes at the stain with a cloth.

>   DAVID
>   Thank you.
>
>   RECEPTIONIST
>   You're in Room 101. You should always keep
>   the dog there. You're excused from to-day's
>   programme, so you can spend the rest of the
>   day however you like.

INT. HOTEL RECEPTION ROOM - DAY

A large room, most of which is empty. In one corner of the room are four desks arranged in a row with some chairs. David gets undressed. He leaves his clothes, his wallet, his wedding band and his mobile phone with the 70-Year-Old Waiter and a MAID, who stores them in a box. Sitting on chairs in just their underwear are the rest of the people who arrived with David on the coach.

The maid takes David's bag, opens it and takes a look inside.

>   MAID
>   I am afraid you cannot keep any of your
>   personal belongings. We will provide you
>   with everything you need as far as gar-
>   ments, accessories and shoes are concerned.
>   Shoe size please?
>
>   DAVID
>   44 and a half.
>
>   MAID
>   44 or 45. There are no half sizes.
>
>   DAVID
>   45.

They give him a pair of black shoes, a pair of brown shoes and a pair of flip-flops.

>   MAID
>   Please select a playlist for the sound sys-
>   tem in your room.

There are four playlists to choose from, titled: BEST LOVE SONGS EVER VOL. I, BEST LOVE SONGS EVER VOL. II, BEST LOVE SONGS EVER VOL. III, and BEST LOVE SONGS EVER VOL. IV. David pauses to think.

>   DAVID
>   BEST LOVE SONGS EVER Volume Three, please.

                    MAID
     If you need a haircut, call reception one
     day ahead. Smoking is not allowed. That
     way you'll be able to run for longer during
     the hunt without getting tired, and your
     breath won't smell when you kiss. Enjoy your
     stay.

                    DAVID
     Thank you.

                    BISCUIT WOMAN
     Excuse me, if we need a haircut we must call
     reception for an appointment the day before?

                    MAID
     That's right.

                    BISCUIT WOMAN
     Great.

INT. ROOM 101 - MORNING

The room is typical of a nice hotel. It has a single bed,
a single chair beside a small table and a teacup upturned
on its saucer on the table. There is also the latest tech-
nology TV set and sound system. The floor is carpeted.

                    FEMALE V.O.
     His room number was 101. A tranquilliser gun
     was hanging on the wall above his bed.
     On the bedside table were 20 tranquilliser
     darts.

We watch David enter the room in just his underwear. He
holds the dog by its leash. David looks around the room:
a single bed and a wardrobe beside it. Hanging on the
wall above the bed is a tranquilliser gun. There are tranquilliser darts on the bedside table. David takes the
leash off the dog and looks around.

                    FEMALE V.O. (CONT'D)
     Inside the wardrobe were four identical grey
     trousers, four identical white and blue
     button down shirts, a belt, socks, under-
     wear, a blazer, a striped tie, a black
     plastic watch, a pair of sunglasses, a white
     bathrobe and a cologne for men. He thought
     they must probably give the women the same
     cologne but for women. Maybe the man with
     the bad leg could become his friend. But not
     if he was courting the same woman he was.
     Then they'd surely fight, he thought. He'd
     never reach the point where he'd kill him
     but they'd fight, that's for sure.

David opens the wardrobe. Inside the wardrobe are four identical grey trousers, four identical white and blue button down shirts, a belt, socks, underwear, a blazer,
a striped tie, a black plastic watch, a pair of sunglasses, a white bathrobe and a cologne for men. David sits
down on the edge of the bed. He reads the leaflet. The dog
looks out the window.

INT. ROOM 101 - AFTERNOON

David, now dressed, looks out the window. The coach pulls up outside the hotel entrance. Men and women, residents of the hotel, climb out of the coach carrying unconscious people. They dump the limp bodies next to the 70-Year-Old Waiter, who counts them, and the Maid takes notes in a folder. The phone rings. David answers it.

DAVID

Yes?

BISCUIT WOMAN (O.S.)

Good afternoon.

DAVID

Good afternoon.

BISCUIT WOMAN (O.S.)

I'm calling from Room 180. I'm 45 years old but I look 40 because I follow a healthy diet and I've worked out ever since I was young. How about you?

David answers, but hasn't yet figured out who he's talking to.

DAVID

I'm 40 years old.

BISCUIT WOMAN (O.S.)

How was your day?

DAVID

Fine.

The dog barks.

BISCUIT WOMAN (O.S.)

You have a dog?

DAVID

Yes.

BISCUIT WOMAN (O.S.)

I love dogs very much and they take to me right away. I think we're going to get along famously. Do you like butter biscuits?

Now he gets it.

DAVID

Yes.

BISCUIT WOMAN (O.S.)

I don't just like them, I like them a lot. Let's have tea or coffee sometime with biscuits. You sound like a very interesting person. Feel free to call me whenever you like, morning or night, until 10 o'clock. If I don't answer, try again. I take these pills for my thyroid gland, they told me they might make me drowsy. My room number is 180, so my phone number is 180. I have to go now because I'm feeling sleepy. We'll talk later. Goodbye.

                         DAVID
            Goodbye.

He hangs up and stands there staring at the phone for
a minute.

INT. ROOM 101 - AFTERNOON

David sleeps in his clothes on the bed. The dog sleeps
on the floor. The HOTEL MANAGER and her HUSBAND enter.
David wakes up, fixes his hair a little. The 70-Year-Old
Waiter and the Maid follow them in. The Hotel Manager
is a woman of around 40. She is dressed formally and her
hair is carefully styled.

                    HOTEL MANAGER
            Good afternoon. I am the Hotel Manager and
            this gentleman is my partner. You're one
            of the lucky ones because your room is one
            of our superior rooms. That means it has
            a view.

The Hotel Manager sits on the only chair and her Husband
stands beside her. They resemble the paintings on the lobby wall, only in reverse.

                    HOTEL MANAGER (CONT'D)
            Did you read the leaflet?

                         DAVID
            I did, yes.

                    HOTEL MANAGER
            Very good. The fact that you'll turn into
            an animal if you don't manage to fall in
            love with another person during your stay
            here is not something that should upset
            you, or get you down. Just think, as an
            animal you'll have a second chance to find
            a companion. But even then you must be very
            careful. You'll need to find a companion
            who is the same type of animal as you are.
            A wolf and a penguin could never live
            together, nor could a camel with a hippo-
            potamus. That would be absurd. Think about
            it. But there are certain combinations in
            particular that are worst of all - for
            example a bear with a fish, or a lion with
            an antelope, or a fox with a chicken.
            I realise that this discussion is a little
            unpleasant for you but I have a duty to
            prepare you psychologically for every pos-
            sible outcome. Have you decided what animal
            you would like to be if you end up alone?

                         DAVID
            A lobster.

                    HOTEL MANAGER
            Why a lobster?

David seems to have thought this through rather well.

                    DAVID
          Because a lobster lives to be over 100
          years old, has blue blood just like an
          aristocrat and stays fertile all its life.
          And I like the sea very much. I waterski
          and swim quite well, ever since I was a
          teenager.

                    HOTEL MANAGER
          I must congratulate you. Usually the first
          thing people think of is a dog and that's
          why the world is full of dogs. Very few
          choose to become unusual animals, which is
          why they are endangered. Rarely does some-
          one choose to be a tuna fish, due to the
          dangers it faces, or a polar bear, due
          to its adverse living conditions. A lobster
          is an excellent choice. One more thing,
          before we leave.

The Hotel Manager signals to the 70-Year-Old Waiter and
the Maid. They take David's arm, twist it behind his back
and bring out a special leather accessory consisting of a
belt and a bracelet linked together. They fasten the belt
around his waist and the bracelet around his wrist, so
that his hand is held tight behind his back and he cannot
move his arm. The belt buckle in front is then locked with
a small key, so that he cannot take it off.

                    HOTEL MANAGER (CONT'D)
          This is to make you realise how easy life
          is when there are two of something instead
          of just one. We forget this from time
          to time. The handcuff and the belt will
          be removed at the same time tomorrow. But
          that's enough for today. I imagine it
          was a trying day. Good evening and enjoy
          your stay.

They leave and close the door behind them. David looks
down at the belt and bracelet.

INT. ROOM 101 - NIGHT

David has placed his toothbrush on the bathroom sink and
tries to squeeze toothpaste onto it. He then tries to
screw the plastic cap back onto the toothpaste tube, and
fails over and over again. He finally brushes his teeth.

INT. ROOM 101 - NIGHT

David stands beside his bed. He tries to pull off his
trousers with the belt still on in order to free his hand.
He struggles. He lies down, sucks in his belly and pushes
his trousers down. After much effort, he manages to free
one leg.

INT. ROOM 101 - MORNING

David sleeps in his underwear. He has managed to take his
trousers off, which are still attached to his wrist by the
bracelet. He is woken up by the music of a very well-known
love song, "A Groovy Kind of Love" by Phil Collins. He
looks at his watch. David gets up and sits on the side of
the bed. He fixes his hair with both hands, lifting up the
trousers on his wrist as he does so. He puts water in a
plate for the dog. Puts some Tiger Balm on his lower back.

INT. BREAKFAST ROOM - MORNING

David enters the breakfast room wearing his trousers as normal. The breakfast room is very tidy and clean. David walks quickly, trying to find an empty table to sit at. Everybody looks at him as he walks by. He looks straight ahead the whole time. All the men wear the same clothes. All the women do too. They all sit alone. There is only one chair at each table in the room. He sees Limping Man, who was with him on the coach. He too has his arm tied behind his back. All the new arrivals wear this same accessory.

                  FEMALE V.O.
   His first day was one he would never forget
   as long as he lived. Near his table at
   breakfast sat a young woman with her head
   tilted back. Later he would learn that
   she often got nosebleeds. Next to her sat
   her best friend. The woman who was with him
   on the coach offered a biscuit to a man
   drinking a Campari and soda for breakfast.
   He then looked behind him and saw a man and
   a woman he would meet in due course, and
   some others he would never meet during his
   stay at the hotel.

We see NOSEBLEED WOMAN, her BEST FRIEND who stares at her, Biscuit Woman (with one hand tied behind her back), CAMPARI MAN, LISPING MAN and HEARTLESS WOMAN, characters we will get to know later. Lisping Man is around 50 years old and Heartless Woman is around 35 and very beautiful. David spreads butter and marmalade on a slice of bread with one hand and eats. Limping Man and Lis-ping Man come up to his table.

                  LIMPING MAN
   I've decided to go for a walk outside with
   my new friend. Let me introduce you.
   This is Robert, he stays in the room next
   to mine and has a lisp.

David puts down his cup of coffee and offers his hand to Lisping Man. They shake hands awkwardly because of his restraining device.

                  DAVID
   Pleased to meet you. I'm staying in
   Room 101.

                  LIMPING MAN
   Would you like to join us?

                  DAVID
   Why not?

EXT. BEACH - MORNING

Limping Man, David and Lisping Man sit on the pier. Three yachts are seen in the bay in the distance. The pier is guarded by TWO ARMED WAITERS.

                  LISPING MAN
   She's much older than he is - you know
   that, right?

                              DAVID
            Yes.

                              LIMPING MAN
            Yes.

                              LISPING MAN
            When Melanie was with Don, I could under-
            stand what brought them together clearly.
            He was more her age and their hair colour
            really matched, as they were both straw-
            berry blond. But now with Antonio, it's re-
            ally strange, it doesn't really make sense.
            I mean, he's much darker than she is and,
            as you know, much younger.

                              LIMPING MAN
            Maybe there's something we don't know. I've
            heard he has his own business, he sells
            this aftershave, you know, named after him-
            self.

                              DAVID
            Maybe she has an aftershave or a cologne
            named after her too.

                              LISPING MAN
            Maybe. I don't know. What I do know is
            that these two are a shining example
            to us all because their relationship is
            a really long-lasting one. Whenever I
            feel down, I think of these two and tell
            myself that I'm going to make it, that
            everything's going to be alright. I keep
            hold of this thought and I know that
            my days at this place are numbered. One
            of these days it's going to be me on
            one of those three yachts.

                              DAVID
            What are those yachts?

                              LISPING MAN
            It's the final ordeal before letting you
            go, and the hardest one. 15 days of vaca-
            tion, just the couples, alone. Haven't you
            read the leaflet?

                              DAVID
            I have.

INT. LECTURE HALL - MIDDAY

The new arrivals at the hotel sit on seven chairs on
stage. David sits last in line. There is a wireless microphone which they each take to speak. Behind the po-
dium stands the Hotel Manager. Her Husband stands beside,
and a little behind her.

All the residents are attending the event, including
Heartless Woman, Nosebleed Woman and her Best Friend. They
are all sitting very quietly. Waiters and Maids stand
randomly around the room, in pairs. The 70-Year-old Waiter
and the Maid observe the new residents from the side of
the stage.

                    HOTEL MANAGER
          Room 206, Day 2.

                    LIMPING MAN
          Hello, everyone.

                    LIMPING MAN (V.O.) (CONT'D)
          My mother was left on her own when my
          father fell in love with a woman who was
          better at math than she was. She had a
          postgraduate degree, I think, whereas my
          mother was only a graduate.

EXT. ZOO - DAY

We see Limping Man walking normally, without a limp, in
a zoo and holding a carrier bag. He passes various caged
animals and reaches the wolf enclosure. He takes pieces of raw meat out of the bag and throws them into the
enclosure at various places. The wolves draw close.

                    LIMPING MAN (V.O.)
          I was nineteen at the time. My mother en-
          tered the hotel but didn't make it and was
          turned into a wolf. I really missed her.
          I found out she'd been moved to a zoo. I
          often went there to see her. I'd give her
          raw meat, I knew wolves liked raw meat
          but I couldn't figure out which of the
          wolves was my mother, so I used to give a
          little bit to each of them.

Limping Man climbs up the enclosure fence. The wolves
come over to where the man is. Only two wolves stand motionless and watch from a corner of the enclosure.

                    LIMPING MAN (V.O.)
          One day I decided to enter the enclosure.
          I really missed her and I wanted a hug.
          I climbed the fence and jumped in. All the
          wolves charged at once and attacked me.
          All but two, who stood motionless. My guess
          is that one of those two must have been
          my mother. The zoo guards got to me quite
          quickly and took me to the hospital.
          Thankfully I didn't lose my leg, I just
          have this limp, which is also my defining
          characteristic. My wife died six days
          ago. She was very beautiful and I loved
          her very much. She had a limp too.

We see a ZOO GUARD hosing down the blood in the wolf enclosure. A tiger sleeps in the next cage.

INT. LECTURE HALL - MIDDAY

The audience applauds. Heartless Woman doesn't. Some stand.
The 70-Year-Old Waiter also claps and the Maid gives
him a look. The Hotel Manager waits for the applause to
peter out.

                    HOTEL MANAGER
          Reference letters. 1 - "He is very sensitive
          and a very good friend. I lent him money
          back in 2014 and he paid me back before the
          repayment date." 2 - "John is wonderful.

> He loves kids and is a first-class conver-
> sationalist." Let's move on to our next
> guest. Room 104, Day 2.

The guest from room 104 is one of the women from the coach. She takes the microphone and speaks. She seems very stressed.

> GUEST FROM ROOM 104
> Hello, everyone. This is only my second day
> here but already I feel like a member of a
> wonderful group. My defining characteristic
> is that I have a very beautiful smile.

INT. BALLROOM - EVENING

A big room, cheerfully decorated. The Hotel Manager and her Partner stand on stage singing a love song together as a duet. Both are showing off, trying to impress the audience with their vocal abilities. Some strobe lights hang from the ceiling and there are two tables laden with sandwiches and refreshments. Couples dance. Limping Man and Lisping Man have found partners to dance with. Two women sit at a table: Nosebleed Woman and her Best Friend. A woman sits on her own at the next table. She is Heartless Woman, whom we saw at breakfast. Biscuit Woman enters and goes over to her table.

> BISCUIT WOMAN
> May I join you?

> HEARTLESS WOMAN
> No, you may not. And don't you dare come
> near me again.

> BISCUIT WOMAN
> I'm sorry.

Biscuit Woman goes to the table where Nosebleed Woman and her Best Friend sit.

> BISCUIT WOMAN (CONT'D)
> Can I sit with you?

> NOSEBLEED WOMAN
> Of course. Let me introduce you to my
> best friend.

Biscuit Woman and Nosebleed Woman's Best Friend shake hands.

> NOSEBLEED WOMAN (CONT'D)
> The woman you were talking to, she has no
> feelings whatsoever. Feels nothing at
> all. Just be careful around her, keep your
> distance. Understood?

> BISCUIT WOMAN
> Okay.

> NOSEBLEED WOMAN'S BEST FRIEND
> She's the best hunter in the hotel. Sil-
> ent and very fast. She's the women's record
> holder. 192 captives.

> BISCUIT WOMAN
> Who's the men's record holder?

                    NOSEBLEED WOMAN
          An assistant university professor. He's
          not at the hotel any more. He left in 2009
          after a year here. 323 captives.

David approaches their table and looks at NOSEBLEED WOMAN.

                    DAVID
          Would you like to dance?

                    NOSEBLEED WOMAN
          Sure.

They go to dance. Romantic instrumental music plays.
There are around ten couples on the dance floor. Limping
Man dances with Biscuit Woman.

                    LIMPING MAN
          I think I have to rest a little bit. My leg
          hurts.

                    BISCUIT WOMAN
          That's ok. As soon as you feel better just
          let me know and we can dance again.

Lisping Man and Heartless Woman dance towards the back.

                    LISPING MAN
          What do you think of the newcomers?

                    HEARTLESS WOMAN
          They're all pathetic. That's what I think.

                    LISPING MAN
          David's ok. Seems like a nice guy.

                    HEARTLESS WOMAN
              (without lisping)
          You mean a nice guy.

Nosebleed Woman's nose starts to bleed, staining David's
shirt.

                    NOSEBLEED WOMAN
          I'm sorry, I've got blood on you. But don't
          worry. There are many ways to remove blood
          stains from clothes quite easily. One
          is to wash the item in cold water and then
          rub it with sea salt. Another is to scrub
          the stains with cotton wool dip-ped in
          ammonia. The third way is to use water and
          flour mixed into a paste, like toothpaste,
          especially if the clothes are delicate
          or brightly coloured. But never use hot wa-
          ter on blood. Ever.

David doesn't seem to mind much. An alarm goes off. They
all run from the ballroom.

INT. ROOM 101 - EVENING

David quickly enters his room. He takes the tranquilliser
gun off the wall and loads it. He puts on a coat and
Wellingtons. He leaves the room. The dog looks at him but
doesn't react.

INT. HOTEL COACH - EVENING

David gets into the coach with the others and sits next to Limping Man, who seems very nervous.

Seated further back in the coach, Lisping Man shows Biscuit Woman how to load her gun.

> LIMPING MAN
> I wish I didn't have this limp. I used to be very good at running but not anymore. I'm sure I'll be slower than them.

> DAVID
> If I were you, I'd think of some tricks that use the element of surprise instead of speed.

> LIMPING MAN
> You're right. That's what I'll do.

A glimmer of hope lights his face.

EXT. THE WOODS - EVENING

We see male and female residents of the hotel get off the coach armed with their tranquilliser guns. They run off, holding powerful torches, in different directions to hunt LONERS who live in the woods. Some seem really excited. Others look bored. The waiters and maids who escort them get off the coach and stand in front of the vehicle. The driver switches off the coach headlights. The Maid lights a cigarette and offers one to the 70-Year-Old Waiter.

EXT. THE WOODS - EVENING

Limping Man struggles to run. He tries to climb some rocks but doesn't manage it.

EXT. THE WOODS - EVENING

Heartless Woman spots a YOUNG LONER WOMAN picking and eating nuts off a tree. The Young Loner Woman notices her and starts to run. Heartless Woman chases after her. After a hard chase she catches her and beats her into unconsciousness, then gets up and shoots her with the tranquilliser gun as well.

EXT. THE WOODS - EVENING

Bald Man and another HOTEL GUEST stand over the UNCONSCIOUS BODY of a LONER. They both start to drag the body away in different directions to no avail. They then stop and hit each other.

EXT. THE WOODS - EVENING

David spots a LONER MAN in the distance trying to hide. He takes aim with his gun, shoots and misses. The Loner Man notices him and starts to run. David starts shooting over and over again. He misses and runs after him. After a while David stops, out of breath. He realises he's also out of tranquilliser darts. He sits on a rock. He looks at his watch.

EXT. HOTEL ENTRANCE - NIGHT

The hotel guests are lined up in front of the coach. Biscuit Woman is standing next to Lisping Man, disappointed.

BISCUIT WOMAN
You must show me again how to load the gun. I just couldn't do it. It was so much better with the bows and arrows.

LISPING MAN
Ok.

BISCUIT WOMAN
I can come to your room with my gun whenever it's convenient for you.

LISPING MAN
I would prefer if we meet at the lobby sometime. My room is really a mess.

BISCUIT WOMAN
Ok.

Some of them have unconscious bodies of loners beside them. The Maid, holding a folder, goes to each hotel guest in turn and announces to them how many extra days' stay at the hotel they have earned based on the number of loners they have captured. She first shines a light in their faces and then on the bodies beside each guest. She comes first to Lisping Man.

MAID
Room 186, one loner, one extra day. 38 days' stay left, plus one, 39.

She then goes to Heartless Woman.

MAID (CONT'D)
Room 290, four loners, four extra days. 154 days' stay left, plus four, 158. You know that you don't have to kill them, right?

HEARTLESS WOMAN
I know.

Next is Limping Man.

MAID
Room 206. The days of your stay remain unchanged.

She then goes to David. He has taken no prisoners.

MAID (CONT'D)
Room 101. The days of your stay remain unchanged.

The Maid moves on.

MAID (CONT'D)
Room 302?

The 70-Year-Old Waiter who also escorted the hotel guests to the hunt answers her.

                    70-YEAR-OLD WAITER
          He never returned. Either he was lost in
          the woods, was captured or he escaped.

                    MAID
          If he doesn't show up by noon tomorrow,
          arrange for Room 302 to be cleaned and pre-
          pared.

                    70-YEAR-OLD WAITER
          Alright.

EXT. BREAKFAST ROOM - MORNING

David sits alone at a table. He drinks milk. Behind
him the Hotel Manager, her Husband and the Maid are speaking with Lisping Man. The 70-Year-Old Waiter brings a
toaster and places it on the table.

                    HOTEL MANAGER
          Is your room number 186?

                    LISPING MAN
          Yes it is.

                    HOTEL MANAGER
          I imagine you know that masturbation is not
          permitted in the rooms or in any other area
          of the hotel.

                    LISPING MAN
          Yes.

                    HOTEL MANAGER
          And yet it has been brought to my attention
          that you continue to do it.
                    [to the Maid]
          Had he ejaculated when you found him?

                    MAID
          We don't know. There was water everywhere in
          the bathroom because he'd just had a shower,
          so we couldn't tell.

                    HOTEL MANAGER
          Were you looking at a photograph while you
          were masturbating?

                    LISPING MAN
          Yes.

                    HOTEL MANAGER
          What did the photograph show?

                    LISPING MAN
          A naked woman on a horse in the country.

                    HOTEL MANAGER
          Do you have it with you?

                    LISPING MAN
          No. It's in my room.

> HOTEL MANAGER
> If I were in your shoes I wouldn't be
> ogling the naked woman but the horse.
> I'm sure that horse used to be a weak and
> cowardly man, just like you.

Lisping Man does not reply. The Maid and the 70 Year-Old Waiter grab Lisping Man's arms and put one of his hands in the toaster. They turn it on. A couple of seconds later he screams.

> LISPING MAN
> I'm sorry. I'm sorry.

David pours some more milk from the bottle into his glass. His eyes don't move. He doesn't glance back.

INT. LECTURE HALL - EVENING

The Maid and the 70-Year-Old Waiter stand in the middle of the stage. The hotel guests sit and watch. The Hotel Manager talks to the audience with a microphone. Besides her stands her Partner, as usual.

> HOTEL MANAGER
> Good evening, everyone. With the help of
> this reenactment, we'd like to show you
> what it's like when someone lives on their
> own and what it's like when they live with
> someone else.
>   (pause)
> One. Man eats alone.

The 70-Year-Old Waiter opens a folding table on stage and places a plate on it. He pretends to eat and then suddenly chokes, falls off his chair and pretends to die. He then gets up and sits back down on his chair. This time the Maid sits opposite him.

> HOTEL MANAGER (CONT'D)
> Two. Man eats with woman.

The 70-Year-Old Waiter again pretends to eat and choke but this time the Maid gets up, performs the Heimlich manoeuver on him and he recovers. They then hug.

> HOTEL MANAGER (CONT'D)
> Three. Woman walks alone.

The Maid walks across the stage. The 30 year-old Waiter stands in the middle of the stage, blocks her path, pulls down his trousers and pretends to rape her.

> HOTEL MANAGER (CONT'D)
> Four. Woman walks with man.

The 70-Year-Old Waiter and the Maid walk together across the stage and pass in front of the rapist waiter. Nothing happens. The audience applauds.

INT. ROOM 101 - MIDDAY

David throws a ball for his dog to fetch. The dog looks very happy. David doesn't praise the dog when it brings the ball back. The phone rings.

                    DAVID
          Hello? Yes, send them up. Thank you.

David goes to the bathroom and looks at himself in the
mirror. He washes his face and brushes his teeth in a
rush. Someone knocks on the door. David opens the door.
An ELDERLY COUPLE stand outside. They are his parents. He
is hugged first by his FATHER, then by his MOTHER. His
mother then hugs the dog.

                    DAVID'S MOTHER
          Easy now, darling. Look at how he wags his
          tail when he looks at his father. Where's
          your father? Go to your father.

The dog doesn't move. His father goes to him and
strokes him.

                    DAVID'S MOTHER (CONT'D)
          Look at him. He's wagging his tail. That's
          what dogs do when they're happy.

They sit on the edge of the bed.

                    DAVID
          Would you like something to drink? I can
          call room service and order you anything
          you like.

                    DAVID'S MOTHER
          I'd like a glass of sparkling water.

                    DAVID'S FATHER
          The same for me. That's a lovely idea.

                    DAVID
          Hi. I am calling from Room 101 and I would
          like to order 2 glasses of sparkling water
          please. Thank you.

                    DAVID'S FATHER
          This is a very nice room.

                    DAVID
          It's one of their superior rooms. It has
          a very nice view. Go to the window and take
          a look.

                    DAVID'S FATHER
          It's really a very nice view.

                    DAVID
          Mother, go and take a look too.

                    DAVID'S MOTHER
          Really very nice.

They sit back down.

                    DAVID'S FATHER
          It's tragic what's happened to you but
          I think everything will be alright in the
          end. We're both very optimistic. You have
          another 26 days. That's three weeks.
          What am I talking about, that's more than
          three weeks. You should get a haircut as
          soon as you can. You're much more handsome

> with your hair short. Your sister sends her
> regards. She said she'd visit you the
> first chance she gets. She's in Switzerland
> with Mark. They're having a wonderful time.
> Skiing all day. Mark didn't know how to
> ski but he's doing very well. He managed
> to ski down the whole piste all by himself
> on Monday. Your mother told them that they
> have to be careful though. Skiing's no
> laughing matter. You can easily get hurt.

The Maid enters the room bringing the sparkling water David ordered. She places the tray on a small table and leaves. David's parents drink the water down in one go. They then get up and put on their coats. They say their goodbyes at the door.

                   DAVID'S FATHER (CONT'D)
We'll come again soon.

                      DAVID'S MOTHER
We'll come again soon. Give this to your brother later. It's sirloin steak.

                           DAVID
Okay.

David closes the door and gives the dog the sirloin steak.

INT. HOTEL BAR - NIGHT

Limping Man, Lisping Man and David sit alone but at adjacent tables and are having a drink.

                      LIMPING MAN
What they do as soon as you enter the room is to wash your body and your head really well.

                      LISPING MAN
How do you know?

                      LIMPING MAN
My uncle used to know a waiter who worked here.

                      LISPING MAN
No waiter knows the procedure. They're not allowed inside that room.

                      LIMPING MAN
Nevertheless, they peel off the skin - which has become soft due to the water and the soap - and afterwards they remove the heart, the eyes and other vital organs of the body with laser or scalpels. That's the part that hurts the most. The procedure then changes according to the animal one has chosen.

                           DAVID
That totally makes sense. I guess mammals demand a different kind of work than fowls, for example.

                    LIMPING MAN
          Exactly. Afterwards they throw the remain-
          ing parts of the body into the huge metal
          casks behind the hotel's restaurant
          and they distribute the blood to the city's
          hospitals.

                    LISPING MAN
          Why is that?

                    LIMPING MAN
          The blood is used for surgeries for which
          there are no blood donors available.

                    LISPING MAN
          Well, there's another story I've heard
          where you enter a dark room with little
          flashing blue and red lights in the
          ceiling. They make you lie on a bed or
          something, the lights keep flashing and
          that's it. You become an animal.

David tries to change the subject of the discussion. There
are other Hotel guests on other tables sitting alone.

                    DAVID
          New guests arrived yesterday.

                    LIMPING MAN
          Yes, I saw that.

                    DAVID
          I think I saw a woman with a limp.

                    LIMPING MAN
          It's only a sprained ankle. She'll
          be walking normally again in a few days.
          I asked her.

                    DAVID
          That's a shame.

                    LISPING MAN
          That's a shame indeed.

Limping Man looks back down at his glass, moves the ice
around. David tries to find something to say but can't.
They sit silently. The alarm bell goes off. They all get
up and leave the room.

INT. HOTEL COACH - NIGHT

David sits in a seat and looks out the window.

                    FEMALE V.O.
          One day he sat next to the woman with the
          biscuits on the coach. He gazed out the
          window, not looking at anything in particu-
          lar, just trying to avoid talking to her.

Biscuit Woman sits beside him. Behind them are Lisping Man
and Limping Man.

                    BISCUIT WOMAN
          How's Bob?

> DAVID
> He's fine.

David tries to be polite but the pretence is obvious. Although she bores him, he feels sorry for her for some reason.

> BISCUIT WOMAN
> I'd give anything to go for a walk with you and Bob one afternoon.

> DAVID
> The dog's not allowed out of the room, I'm afraid.

> FEMALE V.O.
> There are some excuses that no-one can argue with, he thought. Some excuses are, without doubt, better than others. And that was a really good one.

> BISCUIT WOMAN
> These biscuits are for Bob. I want you to give them to him whenever you want to reward him for something, and tell him they're from me.

> DAVID
> Thank you.

He looks out the window again. She doesn't give up though.

> BISCUIT WOMAN
> Can I come to your room sometime for a chat? I could give you a blow job or you could fuck me. I always swallow after fellatio and I have absolutely no problem with anal sex, if that's your thing. My ex-husband always used to say I had the most beautiful thighs he'd ever seen in his life, but let's not talk about him. I'm in Room 180. My telephone extension number is 180. I hope I catch some loners today because I didn't catch any the last few times. I hope you catch lots too.

> DAVID
> Thank you very much.

> BISCUIT WOMAN
> If I don't find a suitable partner soon I'm going to kill myself by jumping from one of the room balconies. I want you to know that. My room is on the first floor. Room numbers that start with a "1" are on the first floor, those starting with a "2" are on the second floor and so on. So 140 is on the first floor and 308 is on the third floor and 190 is also on the first floor. So I'll have to jump from some room that's high up. 380, for example, or 420, that would be even better.

FEMALE V.O.
When she stopped talking, he stared at her
blankly, not knowing what to say. He then
opened the window, looked out at the woods
and thought once more about how good his
excuse had been.

EXT. THE WOODS - NIGHT

Lisping Man walks carefully through the woods. In the
background we see a few hotel residents firing their tranquilliser guns and some loners running away. The animals
in the woods do not react, as if they are used to the
procedure, as if it is something that happens often and
is not terribly interesting. On the other hand, something
really exciting happens to Lisping Man. He notices a
YOUNG LONER WOMAN hiding behind a tree. He stealthily
approaches her and the woman, realising there's no escape,
starts pleading with him to let her go. The young woman
has a lisp. Lisping man notices it as soon as she starts
speaking. His eyes sparkle.

LISPING YOUNG WOMAN
Please don't shoot me. I'll give you this
rabbit. It'll make a great supper.

Lisping Man shoots her. He leans over her unconscious
body, pushing her hair away from her face so that he can
take a better look at her.

INT. COACH - NIGHT

David and Lisping Man sit together. We hear the cries of
a hotel guest injured during the hunt throughout their
conversation. Biscuit Woman sits behind them and listens
to their conversation. Lisping Young Woman is unconscious
next to them.

DAVID
If you two are so well suited, I'm sure
they'll make an exception.

LISPING MAN
I hope so. It's not just that she can't
pronounce her s's, she's also blonde.
Her hair is the exact same colour as mine.
We'd make a perfect couple.

DAVID
If you're so well suited, I'm sure they'll
make an exception.

EXT. SHOOTING RANGE - MORNING

Hotel guests are shooting at targets, so the room is really noisy. David, Limping Man and Lisping Man sit on
a bench waiting their turn to shoot at a training target
with a gun. Lisping Man looks excited. Limping Man does
not look at Lisping Man, but is listening to what he says.
David seems more involved in the conversation.

LISPING MAN
I spoke with the Hotel Manager and she said
that no one should get involved with a
loner. She said it's dangerous and suggested that if I really love her that much,
the right thing to do is to keep her in my

room as a pet. She suggested I turn her
into a parrot and I agreed. The only problem is I can't open the windows in my
room anymore, or when I open them I can
only open them a little. Yesterday she
flew around the room and around the ceiling
light and hit against the walls and windows, and when I turned the light off she
kept on flying for a little bit and then
stopped. I guess she fell asleep. Have you
thought what animal you want to be if you
don't make it?

                  DAVID
A lobster.

Lisping Man takes a plastic bag out of his jacket pocket.
Inside are various coloured feathers he has plucked
from the bird. His eyes are full of joy as he opens the
bag and shows the feathers to David and Limping Man.

                  LISPING MAN
 It's such a beautiful parrot. It has green,
blue, yellow and red feathers. Take a look.

Limping Man stands up and doesn't even bother to look at
the contents of the bag. He puts his hands into his trou-
ser pockets and his face turns very serious.

                LISPING MAN (CONT'D)
If I don't make it, I'm going to become
a parrot. We'll live together. That's
for sure. Why don't you become parrots
too? Then we'll all be together.

                LIMPING MAN
You're a complete idiot, picking one of
the few animals that can talk when
you have a speech impediment. You'll lisp,
even as an animal.
    [to David]
As for you, they'll catch you and throw you
into a pot of boiling water until you
die and then they'll crack open your claws
with a tool like pliers and they'll suck
out what little flesh you have with their
mouths. You're pathetic, both of you. I'm
not going to be turned into some animal.
I'll come visit you though, with my partner, when we're walking together in some
park or when we're swimming in the sea or
when we're on one of our trips.

Lisping Man punches him in the stomach. Limping Man has
his hands in his pockets, and so doesn't have time to react. David separates them. The waiters do not interfere,
they just watch the fight. As soon as David manages to
calm them down, it's his turn to take a shot at the range.

                TRAINER WAITER
Room 206, please.

Limping Man goes and stands beside the waiter. The waiter
hands him the gun.

TRAINER WAITER (CONT'D)
It's no coincidence that the targets are always shaped like a single person and not a couple.

INT. ROOM 101 - MORNING

The Maid enters. She makes the bed. David watches her every move. He seems on edge. He keeps out of her way while she does what she has to do.

MAID
How many darts did you use yesterday?

DAVID
Twelve.

The Maid leaves twelve tranquilliser darts on the bedside table. She notes something down in a folder.

MAID
Please take off your trousers and sit on the bed.

DAVID
Can we not do this today? It's awful.

MAID
I know. But I'm afraid we have to do it. And you have no idea how much it helps you psychologically in your search for a partner.

David takes off his trousers and sits on the edge of the bed. The Maid sits on his lap and jiggles about. She reaches down to grab his cock every so often. David looks like he is enjoying it against his will. He closes his eyes and lays back. Suddenly she gets up.

MAID (CONT'D)
Today you became erect quicker than on other days. That's good. Have a nice day.

DAVID
Please, just a little bit longer.

The Maid takes her trolley and leaves. David is pathetic and desperate.

DAVID (CONT'D)
That's awful. Just awful.

INT. HOTEL POOL - MORNING

Nosebleed Woman is swimming the backstroke. She is very worried about hitting her head on the edge of the pool, so much so that she often stops to look back and see how far she is from the end before continuing. Taking great care, she finally reaches the end, touching the pool side softly with her hand before pushing off for her next 50 metres, filled with the same anxiety. Limping Man limps up to the pool's edge and dives into the water. He swims up to her. David lies on a lounger by the pool and watches them chat. A couple of other Hotel Guests are swimming in the pool.

LIMPING MAN
Hello.

								NOSEBLEED WOMAN
					Thank you.

Limping Man doesn't hear her response because he's
underwater doing a somersault, so Nosebleed Woman repeats
herself when he surfaces.

								NOSEBLEED WOMAN (CON'D)
					Thank you very much.

								LIMPING MAN
					You're welcome. Do you like to swim
					breaststroke, front crawl, butterfly or
					backstroke?

								NOSEBLEED WOMAN
					I like all the strokes equally.

								LIMPING MAN
					You know, I love breaststroke. No, really,
					my friends often tease me and say, "Stop
					swimming breaststroke all the time!" and
					then they laugh.

								NOSEBLEED WOMAN
					Breaststroke is great. Excellent exercise
					for the back.

Nosebleed Woman turns her head away to the left. When
Limping Man is certain she can't see him, he purpose-
ly knocks his head on the side of the pool and his nose
starts to bleed. He acts as if nothing has happened.

								LIMPING MAN
					When swimming breaststroke, men shouldn't
					wear swim shorts as it really limits
					movement in the buttocks. But you knew
					that, didn't you?

He shows her his breaststroke kick.

								NOSEBLEED WOMAN
					I think your nose is bleeding.

								LIMPING MAN
					Really? Oh no, not again. This happens to
					me all the time. It's very, very annoying.

								NOSEBLEED WOMAN
					I know. I have a nosebleed problem too.

INT. HOTEL ROOM - NIGHT

David is wearing his tuxedo. There's a knock at the door.
David goes to the door and opens it. Limping Man stands
outside.

								DAVID
					What's the matter?

								LIMPING MAN
					I want to talk to you.

								DAVID
					Have a seat.

                    LIMPING MAN
          I came to say goodbye.

                    DAVID
          I saw what you did. It must have hurt.

The man bangs his nose against the wall and it bleeds.

                    LIMPING MAN
          I'm going to ask you a question and I want
          you to answer me honestly. What's worse,
          to die of cold and hunger in the woods, to
          become an animal that will be killed and
          eaten by some bigger animal, or to have a
          nosebleed from time to time?

                    DAVID
          To become an animal that will be killed and
          eaten by some bigger animal.

                    LIMPING MAN
          Exactly.

                    DAVID
          She doesn't suspect that you're lying?

                    LIMPING MAN
          No.

Limping Man hugs David. He stains his shirt with blood.

                    LIMPING MAN (CONT'D)
          Don't worry about your shirt. Rub it with
          salt or scrub it with ammonia and it'll
          come out right away but whatever you do,
          don't use hot water. See you downstairs.

INT. BALLROOM - NIGHT

All the residents are dressed up. This is obviously
a special occasion. The Hotel Manager, with her Husband
standing next to her, is presenting the new couple:
Limping Man and Nosebleed Woman. They are now formally
together, a confirmed couple. Their life together will
begin with everyone's blessing. It's like an instant
wedding, a non-ritual ceremony.

                    HOTEL MANAGER
          I'm very happy because we have a new cou-
          ple. They met just two days ago but they
          are very much in love and perfectly suited.
          They both have the same problem with their
          noses. They bleed quite suddenly.

The rest of the hotel guests clap. Heartless Woman
doesn't. Nosebleed Woman's Best Friend cries. She realises she is losing her best friend forever and feels abandoned. David hesitates at first, but after a while he
claps too. But he doesn't smile, and seems worried. The
70-Year-Old Waiter holds a velvet cushion with tassels,
with a room key on it. The Hotel Manager hands
the couple the room key.

                    HOTEL MANAGER (CONT'D)
          Tomorrow they will be transferred to a dou-
          ble room with a larger wardrobe and a
          larger bathroom. They will be allowed to

                    use the group sports facilities and to eat
                    together in the restaurant. They will
                    stay in a double room for two weeks, then
                    they'll move to the yachts for another two
                    and we all hope they'll succeed so they
                    can return back to the city as a couple.

The rest of the guests clap once more. Limping Man
takes the microphone. He speaks loudly, with excitement
and joy.

                         LIMPING MAN
                    I'm very happy.

                         NOSEBLEED WOMAN
                    Me too.

                         HOTEL MANAGER
                    Well done. Congratulations. What are your
                    thoughts on paedophilia?

                         LIMPING MAN
                    I'm against it.

                         NOSEBLEED WOMAN
                    I'm against it.

                         HOTEL MANAGER
                    Good. Do either of you have a serious ill-
                    ness that could prove fatal within the next
                    five years?

                         LIMPING MAN
                    No.

                         NOSEBLEED WOMAN
                    No.

                         HOTEL MANAGER
                    Very good. The course of your relationship
                    will be monitored closely by our staff
                    and by me personally. If you notice any
                    problems, any fighting or tension between
                    you which you cannot resolve yourselves
                    for whatever reason, you will be assigned
                    children. That usually helps. A lot.

The couple leave the room, waving the audience goodbye.
Lisping Man is moved, but slightly jealous. David is
sceptical.

EXT. CHILDREN'S AREA - AFTERNOON

David, Nosebleed Woman, her Best Friend and Limping Man
are looking at some children locked behind some railings
in a large enclosure. They all wear identical clothes:
tracksuits. Most of them are playing. One of the children
comes up to them.

                         CHILD
                    Hello. My parents split up two years ago.
                    They are both animals now. I'm ten years
                    old. I'm very good at algebra and even bet-
                    ter at geometry. If you choose me, I'm
                    100% sure you won't be disappointed. I'm
                    seriously thinking of going to study at
                    the university. Come closer.

Limping Man goes closer. The child strokes Limping Man's cheek and hair.

> CHILD (CONT'D)
> I love you so much, Daddy. Don't be sad, Daddy, everything will be fine, you'll see. I love you so much. You're so strong, stronger than any of my classmates' dads. Here you are, Daddy, here's that cold beer you asked for.

David, Nosebleed Woman, her Best Friend and Limping Man leave. The child can be heard from afar.

> CHILD (CONT'D)
> Look, Daddy, I can ride my bike with no hands. If you don't pick me, I hope you die alone and that they find your body days after you die.

> DAVID
> I'm sure you won't need a child. You'll get on just fine.

INT. HOTEL THERMAL SUITE - AFTERNOON

Nosebleed Woman's Best Friend and David are in bathrobes, lying on loungers. David looks at her, notices her figure, her hands, her hair. David's voice grows softer. His tone changes.

> DAVID
> You have really nice hair.

> NOSEBLEED WOMAN'S BEST FRIEND
> I know. Look.

Nosebleed Woman's Best Friend flicks her head to show David how smoothly her hair moves.

> DAVID
> How do you like mine?

> NOSEBLEED WOMAN'S BEST FRIEND
> Well, I think you have quite dry hair. The colour is ok though, and the important thing is that you are not bald. However, when it comes to men, baldness is a possibility even if your hair is thick like yours. Hair loss is a sneaky thing, you can't predict it - it's a matter of genes and a million other factors. Is your father bald?

> DAVID
> No, he isn't. And even if I someday lose my hair, there are ways that I can get my hair back. I can get a hair transplant.

> NOSEBLEED WOMAN'S BEST FRIEND
> They are rarely successful. You can always tell when someone has had a hair transplant. Nice hair is not something you can get, it's something you're born with. And the fact that your father isn't bald shouldn't put you at ease. Maybe you

>   have your grandfather's genes or the genes
>   of another bald relative of yours.

Her strictness on the hair issue ends their conversation and David can't muster the courage to have another try.

INT. HOTEL MANAGER'S OFFICE - MORNING

The Hotel Manager, her Partner, Nosebleed Woman and her Best Friend sit at a table. The Best Friend is crying. Nosebleed Woman is not.

>   HOTEL MANAGER
>   Today is your last day. As is customary,
>   you can choose how you would like to spend
>   your last night. What I always say in
>   these situations is that it would be wise
>   to choose something you cannot do as an
>   animal, like read a work of classic lit-
>   erature or sing a song you really like. It
>   would be silly if you chose, for example,
>   a walk in the grounds or to have sexual
>   intercourse with someone, because these are
>   things you can also do as an animal. But
>   first, your best friend would like to read
>   something she wrote for you that is really
>   very touching.

Nosebleed Woman unfolds a sheet of paper.

>   NOSEBLEED WOMAN
>   We always sat together at school and when-
>   ever I had a problem I talked to you
>   about it because you always gave the best
>   advice. When we didn't manage to find dance
>   partners at the school prom, the fact that
>   we were together at that difficult mo-
>   ment gave me strength. I'm sorry things
>   have come to this. I'm sure that if you had
>   a few more days you'd find someone, just
>   like I did, because you're an admirable
>   person and you have very beautiful hair and
>   very nice breasts. I was always jealous of
>   your hair, you know that. You were, are,
>   and always will be my best friend, and I'll
>   think of you often, and I'll always wear
>   those silver earrings you gave me for my
>   birthday. I'll miss you, and however many
>   new girlfriends I make in a few days when
>   I move back into town, I don't think
>   I'll find another as true or as beautiful
>   as you.

Nosebleed Woman's Best Friend gets up and slaps her. Nosebleed Woman's nose is bleeding from the blow.

>   NOSEBLEED WOMAN'S BEST FRIEND
>   I'd like to watch the film "Stand By Me"
>   with River Phoenix, Kiefer Sutherland and
>   Richard Dreyfuss. Alone.

INT. ROOM 101 - DAY

David looks out of his room window. The Maid holds a pony by its reins. She opens the gate to the hotel grounds and sets the pony free. Nosebleed Woman and Limping Man hug in the hotel entrance and wave goodbye to the pony.

The pony doesn't run off. It just stands there, swishing its beautiful tail. The room phone rings. The display reads 180. He doesn't pick up.

> ANSWERING MACHINE
> Room 101. Please leave a message after the tone.

EXT. GOLF COURT - DAY

David is playing golf by himself.

> FEMALE V.O.
> When I was at the hotel, I never much left my room. Hardly ever. I went there around four years ago. From the very first day, I knew there was no one there who interested me.

EXT. TENNIS COURT - DAY

David holds a bag of golf clubs and watches A COUPLE playing tennis one-on-one in the court from behind the wire fence. They're having fun, they yell and kiss. David is fixated by them.

> FEMALE V.O.
> I used to listen to a lot of French music back then, and no one else listened to French music there. I stayed for 19 days. I let a waiter fuck me in order to help me escape. After he'd fucked me he said that he wouldn't let me go and that I'd better just go back to my room, and quick. I killed him and left. I also killed a resident who tried to stop me leaving because he said he liked me.

EXT. HOTEL GROUNDS - DAY

David heads back towards his room carrying his golf equipment. He sees a crowd of people. Biscuit Woman lies on the ground, covered in blood. She isn't dead and is screaming in pain. David runs towards the crowd. He sees the injured woman lying on the ground and shuts his eyes. He turns away as he can't stand to see her suffer. He spots Heartless Woman and instantly changes his facial expression. He tries hard to look calm and indifferent.

> DAVID
> What happened?

> HEARTLESS WOMAN
> She jumped from the window of Room 180. There's blood and biscuits everywhere.

> DAVID
> I hope she dies right away. On second thought, I hope she suffers quite a bit before she dies. I just hope her pathetic screams can't be heard from my room because I'm thinking about having a lie down and I need peace and quiet. I was playing golf and I'm quite tired and the last thing I need is a women dying slowly and loudly.

                    HEARTLESS WOMAN
          I can't hear you with all this screaming.
          We'll talk some other time when it's quiet-
          er. Bye.

Heartless Woman leaves. David turns and watches her leave. TWO WAITERS arrive with a stretcher.

INT. ROOM 101 - AFTERNOON

David plays the message Biscuit Woman left on his answering machine before she attempted suicide. The incident has obviously upset him. There's a hint of regret in his face. The dog stands beside him, as if listening to the message too.

                    BISCUIT WOMAN
               (MESSAGE ON ANSWERING MACHINE)
          Hello. You're probably in the bathroom,
          that's why you can't hear the phone
          ring. There's nothing better than a cold
          shower in the morning.
               (pause)
          I'll call again a little later when you've
          finished your shower so we can chat.

He pushes play to hear it again. The dog wanders off.

EXT. JACUZZI - EVENING

Heartless Woman sits alone in the Jacuzzi. She drinks a Martini. David goes towards her. He seems confident. He gets into the Jacuzzi, smiling at her. Heartless Woman looks at him but doesn't react. They don't talk for awhile. Heartless Woman takes the olive from her drink and pops it in her mouth. She chokes. Her face turns red. Her head falls back and her body jolts about in the water. David does not react. After a while she stops her charade.

                    HEARTLESS WOMAN
          I think we're a match.

                    DAVID
          Yes, I think so too. Would you like for us
          to live as a couple from now on?

                    HEARTLESS WOMAN
          Yes. We'll inform the reception desk in the
          morning.

                    DAVID
          Great.

INT. BALLROOM - NIGHT

The Hotel Manager, with her Husband standing next to her, presents David and Heartless Woman with the key to a double room and wishes them the best of luck. Handshakes, smiles and hugs. Same ceremony as with Limping Man and Nosebleed Woman.

INT. DOUBLE ROOM 202 - NIGHT

David, Heartless Woman and the dog enter the room. This room isn't much bigger than the old one but there is a double bed and two bathrobes in the closet. Heartless

Woman gives the dog a plate with water. The dog laps up the water. David looks happy. He checks the bed and the sheets, he takes his clothes off and sits on the chair.

DAVID
Do you normally sleep on the left or the right side of the bed?

HEARTLESS WOMAN
The left. You?

DAVID
The right. Perfect.

They sit down on their respective sides of the bed. David takes off his trousers. Heartless Woman sits on his lap and jiggles about, just like the Maid used to do. She reaches down to grab his cock every so often. Eventually they start having sex. David is behind her. During intercourse he whispers "mmm" and Heartless Woman stops and turns to look at him.

HEARTLESS WOMAN
What was that sound? Did you say something?

DAVID
No.

HEARTLESS WOMAN
Do you mind if we fuck in a position where I can see your face?

DAVID
Sure.

HEARTLESS WOMAN
Turn the light on please, so I can see you better.

David turns the light on and they carry on having sex, during which he tries desperately not to grimace or show signs of overexcitement. She looks him straight in the eye to see if he makes any facial expressions. During his orgasm, David tries hard to remain cold. This is the most difficult part of the process. His face is sweaty, his eyes wide open. Heartless Woman, on the other hand, is naturally expressionless. As soon as they are done, they get dressed.

DAVID
Should I turn off the light or would you like to read?

HEARTLESS WOMAN
I'd like to read. Does the light bother you?

DAVID
No. I'm not bothered by light or noise. I'm a deep sleeper.

Heartless Woman reads. David gets under the covers and turns his back to her. He then turns again and he puts his arm around her waist. He closes his eyes and sleeps.

Heartless Woman eyes him suspiciously.

EXT. HOTEL BEACH - EVENING

David and Heartless Woman are out for a walk. The couple walks hand in hand. They meet Limping Man, who is out walking with Nosebleed Woman and a LITTLE GIRL, ELIZABETH.

LIMPING MAN
Good evening.

DAVID
Good evening.

LIMPING MAN
Congratulations.

DAVID
Thank you.

LIMPING MAN
This is our daughter. Her name is Elizabeth. Elizabeth, give the nice man a kiss. He's a friend of mine.

ELIZABETH goes up to David. He does not bend down to be kissed.

DAVID
The last thing I want right now is a kiss from a silly little girl.

They stand there a little, motionless and then David kicks the child on her shin. She bursts into tears and Nosebleed Woman takes her into her arms.

DAVID (CONT'D)
Don't cry, Elizabeth. You should thank me, now you'll have a limp and be more like your father.

David looks at Limping Man with contempt as he stays motionless, looking slightly guilty for some reason. David and Heartless Woman leave with the dog.

HEARTLESS WOMAN
You should have punched her in the face too, and bloodied her nose and then said, "Don't cry, Elizabeth. You should thank me, now your nose is bloody and you'll be even more like your father."

DAVID
You're right. Why didn't I think of that?

INT. DOUBLE ROOM 202 - MORNING

David wakes up. Heartless Woman stands over him in quite a threatening way.

HEARTLESS WOMAN
Good morning.

DAVID
Good morning.

                    HEARTLESS WOMAN
          I killed your brother. I left him to die
          very slowly. He may not be dead yet, even
          as we speak. I was kicking him for ages.

She shows him her leg. Her shoe is covered in blood.
David tries very hard not to show his true feelings —
he's devastated but pretends that he's indifferent to
what's happened.

                    DAVID
          It doesn't matter.

                    HEARTLESS WOMAN
          He whined a little. A strange kind of bark.
          Something like this. "Woof ow-woof." It
          must've been from the pain. You didn't hear
          anything?

                    DAVID
          No.

                    HEARTLESS WOMAN
          You really are a deep sleeper. Would you
          like some coffee?

                    DAVID
          I'd love some. As soon as I wash my face
          and brush my teeth though.

David goes to the bathroom.

                    HEARTLESS WOMAN
          Right. I can't wait to hear the story you
          promised to tell me last night, about
          that student of yours at the university and
          his awful final project.

                    DAVID
          It's really a very funny story. His name
          was Ryess. R-Y-E-S-S. Ryess.

David splashes water on his face and then finally
bursts into tears. Heartless Woman enters the bathroom
and slaps him.

                    DAVID (CONT'D)
          These aren't tears. It's just water.

                    HEARTLESS WOMAN
          I knew you were lying. I can't understand
          why you did it when you know as well
          as anyone that a relationship cannot be
          built on a lie. We're going to the
          Hotel Manager right now and you'll get
          the punishment you deserve.

                    DAVID
          What's the punishment for this?

                    HEARTLESS WOMAN
          They turn you into the animal no one wants
          to be. You know which one.

                    DAVID
          Yes. I know.

INT. HOTEL CORRIDORS - EVENING

David and Heartless Woman are walking around to find the Hotel Manager. She holds him by the hair. The pain is visible on his face. David suddenly punches her in the stomach and runs away. She gets up after a few seconds and runs down the stairs.

INT. HOTEL FIRST-FLOOR CORRIDOR - EVENING

Heartless Woman reaches the first-floor corridor and tries each door one by one. She sees a door slightly ajar. She pushes it open and enters. She sees a FEMALE HOTEL GUEST giving a WAITER a blow job. A MALE HOTEL GUEST is also giving a SECOND WAITER a blowjob.

INT. HOTEL STAIRS - EVENING

Heartless Woman exits the room, walks down the corridor and goes up to the second floor. She is absolutely cool, she doesn't look angry or nervous, just determined.

INT. HOTEL SECOND-FLOOR CORRIDOR - EVENING

Heartless Woman sees the Maid in the middle of the corridor holding a tray with a glass of Campari and soda.

>MAID
>I saw a man running back that way. He looked frantic.

As soon as Heartless Woman turns back, David emerges from one of the rooms with a tranquilliser gun and shoots her. The Maid leaves the glass of Campari next to Campari Man, who is also unconscious inside the room, and then helps David lift Heartless Woman.

>FEMALE V.O.
>At first he wanted to kill her in some horrible and painful way, like the death she had inflicted on his brother. He thought about kicking her in the stomach over and over again and then stabbing her in the same spot, in the stomach. But then he thought that there wouldn't be much point because she was already unconscious and so she wouldn't feel any pain from the kicks or the knife.

David carefully carries Heartless Woman through the hotel with the help of the Maid. They meet no one in the corridors.

INT. ANIMAL TRANSFORMATION ROOM - EVENING

David and the Maid stand outside the room where they transform people into animals. Heartless Woman is still unconscious on the floor. The Maid unlocks the door using a card and entering a code on a security keypad.

>MAID
>You have to shoot me so they won't suspect I helped you.

David shoots her and she also falls down unconscious. He then drags Heartless Woman into the transformation room and shuts the door behind him.

> FEMALE V.O.
> And so he decided to turn her into an animal. He dragged her to the room that the transformations took place. A hotel maid helped him and he never understood why she did it. I asked him many times what sort of animal he turned her into, but he always gave the same answer: "That's none of your concern." That night he left the hotel, once and for all.

INT. ROOM 202 - EVENING

The Hotel Manager runs to the couple's room with two waiters. She sees the dead dog. She signals to the waiters to set off the alarm.

> HOTEL MANAGER
> The alarm.

> FEMALE V.O.
> He began to run without knowing where he was headed, but he was headed towards us. This was the start of his new life and, back then, he didn't know how much it hurts to be alone, how much it hurts when you cannot reach to rub pain relief cream on your upper back and you are constantly in pain.

EXT. HOTEL GROUNDS - EVENING

David cautiously disappears behind the trees.

III. THE WOODS NEAR THE HOTEL

EXT. THE WOODS - EVENING

David walks very quickly, almost at a jog, as if he is too tired to run but too scared to walk. He stops beside a river. He washes his face and drinks some water. He steams up his glasses with his breath and rubs them clean with his shirt. He continues to walk quickly. He gets tired. The woods are quiet and the only thing you can hear is the birds and the sound of water. Everything is still and there are no animals around that he can actually see.

EXT. THE WOODS- NIGHT

He lies down on the ground but doesn't close his eyes. He just rests but it's obvious that he isn't relaxed at all. He used to visit these woods as a hunter, but now he is the prey.

EXT. THE WOODS - MORNING

David washes his face. Suddenly, he hears a noise. A loner man, LONER SWIMMER, is swimming. David goes towards him.

> DAVID
> Hello.

LONER SWIMMER
Don't shoot. If you shoot me you'll only
gain one extra day. I can tell you
where the others are hiding so you'll have
the chance to gain a whole extra week,
maybe even two.

DAVID
I'm alone. I just escaped from the hotel.

LONER SWIMMER
Okay. I got away about a year ago. Don't
worry. There's nothing to be afraid
of now. So long as they don't catch you.

EXT. THE WOODS - AFTERNOON

Loner Swimmer takes David to the LONER LEADER, a woman
of around 30. She and the rest of the LONERS wear
the same waterproof capes and carry backpacks with their
personal belongings. David seems a little bit lost as
he tries to adapt to the current situation, which he
wasn't prepared for. He looks around amazed at all these
loners who form this autonomous community in the forest.

LONER SWIMMER
I found him out in the woods. He escaped
from the hotel.

LONER LEADER
Are you a doctor, by any chance?

DAVID
No.

LONER LEADER
That's a pity, we need a doctor. We had one
but they caught him a couple of months ago.

DAVID
I'm an architect.

LONER LEADER
That's okay. Are you on any medication
these days we should know of?

DAVID
Well, not really. I have pain in my upper
back and I often put some pain relief cream
on it, but that's all. Nothing important,
really.

LONER LEADER
Alright. So, welcome. You can stay with us
for as long as you like. You can be a
loner until the day you die, there's no
time limit.

DAVID
Thank you very much.

David smiles. Loner Leader gives him an awkward hug.

LONER LEADER
By the way, any romantic or sexual rela-
tions between loners are not permitted and
any such acts are punished. Is that clear?

                    DAVID
          Can I have a conversation with someone?

                    LONER LEADER
          Of course you can, so long as there is no
          flirting or anything like that. That ap-
          plies to dance nights as well. We all dance
          by ourselves, that's why we only play elec-
          tronic music. We have dance nights every
          now and then.

                    DAVID
          That's nice.

EXT. THE WOODS - AFTERNOON

Loner Swimmer, aided by a BANDAGED LONER with bloodied bandages over his mouth, gives David a waterproof cape, a portable CD player, a pocket-sized game of solitaire, the book "Of Mice and Men" by John Steinbeck and a knife. David realizes that he's going to be a proper member of this group. As these changes are taking place, David acts in a mechanical way, without really thinking where all this will lead him. He looks at Bandaged Loner. There's fresh blood on his bandages.

                    DAVID
          What's wrong with your mouth?

                    LONER SWIMMER
          He can't talk. He was given the Red Kiss.

                    DAVID
          What's the Red Kiss?

                    LONER SWIMMER
          We slashed his lips with a razor and the
          lips of another loner and we forced them
          to kiss each other. That was a few days
          ago now but the cuts were deep and they're
          still in pain. They were flirting, you
          know. Check if the portable CD player works
          properly, otherwise I'll have to find you
          some new batteries.

Davis presses play on the CD player. Music plays. He pushes the stop button.

                    DAVID
          It works just fine.

EXT. THE WOODS - AFTERNOON

David takes off his shirt and rubs Tiger Balm cream onto his upper back, as far as he can reach. He cannot reach most of his upper back properly.

EXT. THE WOODS - EVENING

Loner Leader watches a pig eating some weeds. She creeps up without making a sound and slips a lead around its neck. They start walking in the woods. Wherever the animal stops, the leader digs into the ground with her hands as if looking for something. She then gets up, wipes the soil off her hands and continues walking the pig.

EXT. THE WOODS - MORNING

The loners stand in rows and exercise. Loner Leader checks their technique, corrects them whenever necessary, and yells at the lazy ones.

> FEMALE V.O.
> That was the first time I saw him. He was exercising three rows behind me. He seemed quite presentable.

We see a woman, whom we'll soon get to know as SHORT-SIGHTED WOMAN, exercising and looking at David. David does what the others do, a little confused but determined at the same time.

> FEMALE V.O. (CONT'D)
> The next day, in the city, I found out that he was shortsighted too, just like me, and I knew for sure that he liked me. That night, in my sleep, I dreamt that we lived in a big house together in the town, with a large, well-lit kitchen, and I was wearing dark blue trousers and a tight cream blouse and he took my clothes off and fucked me up the arse and as he was fucking me, a thug came into the kitchen and took the steak knives from the second drawer and attacked us, stabbing the knives into our bellies one by one. I woke up terrified.

A LONER gets caught in a foothold trap. He screams. The others stop and go near him, but don't help him. They talk amongst themselves and give him advice on how to free himself. David watches. Shortsighted Woman stands behind him.

> LONER LEADER
> Try harder. Pull the trap open with your hands. Positive thinking is everything at times like this. Don't give up. You know, you should've been more careful. Try harder. Or they'll find you and you'll be turned into an animal. A weak one.

Loner Swimmer and the other loners laugh.

> LONER LEADER (CONT'D)
> We must get a move on now. It's really too dangerous to stay here. The hotel guests could be here any minute. If you manage to free yourself, run as fast as you can and come find us. If you manage to free yourself but think that you'll die from the bleeding, go straight to your grave. Have you dug your own grave?

> TRAPPED LONER
> Yes.

> LONER LEADER
> Very good. That's enough for now. Let's split up and spread out. We'll rendezvous tonight at meeting point four.

EXT. THE WOODS - MORNING

David tries to cover himself with leaves, moving slowly and quietly, and smears mud on his face. Silly little things out of inexperience and despair.

Despite his efforts, he is quickly discovered by Lisping Man, who takes aim at David with his tranquilliser gun. David puts his hands up.

> LISPING MAN
> What you did to that woman was dreadful. I can't understand why you would turn her into a dog and then kick her to death.

> DAVID
> She killed my brother. I would have done the same thing if she'd killed you. You're like a brother to me. You're my best friend in the whole world. We didn't speak much but we both knew that in a pinch we'd be at each other's side.

> LISPING MAN
> I don't believe I'm your best friend in the whole world. You used to spend a lot more time with John.

> DAVID
> Who is John?

> LISPING MAN
> John, the Limping Man.

> DAVID
> Oh. I didn't even remember his name. Or his face. You are the one I think of whenever I need a friend. Nevertheless, did John make it?

David is not very convincing. But Lisping Man mellows.

> LISPING MAN
> They're getting ready for the yacht. It all begins next week. Everyone says they're going to make it as they're very well suited and the child will help them get past the arguing and fighting. What time do you get up in the morning?

> DAVID
> Whenever we like. And we eat whatever we like.

> LISPING MAN
> You're not thinking of coming back? You know, if you told the Hotel Manager about your brother she'd probably forgive you.

                    DAVID
          No. It's really nice being on your own.
          There's no one tying you down. You listen
          to music whenever you like, masturbate
          whenever you like, go for walks whenever
          you like, have a chat whenever you like.
          I don't miss companionship at all. I only
          miss you because you were my one true
          friend. Are you going to shoot me?

                    LISPING MAN
          I'm afraid I have to. I only have two
          days left.

David becomes aggressive all of a sudden.

                    DAVID
          What did you say? I can't understand you,
          the way you speak.

                    LISPING MAN
          I'm going to shoot you. I only have two
          days left and I need more time.

                    DAVID
          You really believe another day will make
          a difference? Have you seen how ugly
          you are? You haven't got a chance. If I
          were a woman, I'd...

Lisping Man prepares to shoot him. Shortsighted Woman
jumps out from behind a bush and stabs a knife into
Lisping Man's leg, then David grabs Lisping Man's tranquilliser gun and shoots him.

                    DAVID (CONT'D)
          Thank you.

                    SHORTSIGHTED WOMAN
          Don't tell anyone I helped you. If you want
          to repay me, there is a way. If you
          kill a rabbit, bring it to me to eat. Do
          you promise?

                    DAVID
          Yes.

                    SHORTSIGHTED WOMAN
          Bye.

Shortsighted Woman leaves. David stands still and watches
her walk off through the trees until she disappears. As
soon as he realizes what has just happened, he searches
through the still-unconscious Lisping Man's pockets. He
finds some bird feathers, which he throws away. He strips
off Lisping Man's clothes and takes them with him, along
with his gun and shoes.

EXT. A CLEARING IN THE WOODS - MORNING

The Waiter-Driver, the 30-Year-Old Waiter and the Maid,
who joined them for the journey, sit outside the coach.
The residents of the Hotel are heard in the distance
hunting loners. The Maid picks up a bag and slings it
over her back.

                    MAID
          I'm going to go hunting for truffles.
          They're delicious and quite rare. A kilo
          can fetch a lot of money.

                    30-YEAR-OLD WAITER
          You're going to need a pig. They're impos-
          sible to find otherwise.

                    MAID
          I know.

                    WAITER-DRIVER
          Don't be long. We have to take them back in
          50 minutes.

                    MAID
          Okay.

EXT. THE WOODS - MORNING

The Maid walks and stops under a tree. She looks left and right, as if she's waiting for someone. She then looks at her watch. Loner Leader appears. The two women start speaking in French.

                    MAID
          Good morning.

                    LONER LEADER
          Morning. Did you bring the stuff I asked
          for?

                    MAID
          The gun is in the bag, as is the key to
          the small door. The numbers of the double
          rooms are in this blue folder. Try not to
          lose the key cards. I suggest tomorrow,
          Saturday, because after the dance everyone
          is quite tired and many of the staff are
          off work on weekends.

                    LONER LEADER
          What about the shampoo?

                    MAID
          I forgot it. I'll bring you two bottles
          next time.

                    LONER LEADER
          You're terrific, you know that?

The Maid doesn't seem happy, despite the compliment.

                    LONER LEADER (CONT'D)
          Please make a note of the shampoo so you
          don't forget it.

                    MAID
          I have to tell you something.

                    LONER LEADER
          What is it?

                    MAID
          This will be my last mission. I can't take
          it anymore. I can't live in that horrible
          house with that fat dentist. He's always
          asking whether I've flossed and forces me
          to brush my teeth after every meal, however
          small. The other day he kissed me on the
          cheek. When all this is over I'm going to
          kill him in his dentist's chair. I'm going
          to shove the drill into his belly.

The Maid sits on a rock and covers her face with her
hands. It looks like she's crying, but she's not.

                    LONER LEADER
          Alright. When we're done with the big night
          we've got planned, you can come live with
          us and I'll find another insider. I doubt
          I'll find anyone as helpful and efficient
          as you are. But I must respect your wishes.
          Just be patient for a few more days and
          don't forget to take your birth-control
          pills. Okay?

                    MAID
          Thank you.

                    LONER LEADER
          No. We thank you. You are brilliant.

Loner Leader hugs the Maid.

EXT. THE WOODS - EVENING

Loners sit around the woods and rest after the hunt.
Loner Swimmer eats fruit, Shortsighted Woman listens to
music on her headphones, Bandaged Loner reads a book.
Beside him sits a female loner who also has bandages on
her mouth - she's probably the other loner punished with
the Red Kiss torture. David sits next to Loner Leader.
She rubs a hydrating cream onto her hands and face. She
offers some to David but he declines with a shake of
his head.

                    LONER LEADER
          Tomorrow we're going into town. We're go-
          ing to buy some new books as some people
          have been complaining that they've read the
          same book two or three times over. Also,
          someone lost the second volume of "Crime
          and Punishment" during a chase and lots of
          people have read the first part and are
          waiting to see what happened next. You can
          come, if you like.

                    DAVID
          Thank you. I'll come.

                    LONER LEADER
          Excellent. Then you should clean up. We
          must look like very decent, presentable
          couples tomorrow. Make sure you cut your
          nails, clean the dirt off your head and
          comb your hair.

                    DAVID
          Should I put some aftershave on?

                         LONER LEADER
                No, that won't be necessary.

EXT. THE WOODS, TREE HOLLOW - NIGHT

Loner Leader pulls a plastic bag out of a tree hollow
and takes some "civilian" clothes from inside. She hands
David a suit.

                         LONER LEADER
                Hope it fits.

                         DAVID
                Thank you.

David tries on the clothes. The suit actually fits.

EXT. THE CITY - MORNING

Four loners now dressed in suits come out of the woods.
They walk down the road towards the city. They reach
a typical urban environment. Couples, cars, buses, kids,
shops. David has his arm around Shortsighted Woman and
Loner Leader has her arm around Loner Swimmer. They look
like office workers. They walk through the town and enter
a shopping centre. They seem happy. They stare at the
shop windows, then browse random things like nail polish,
paint brushes, cotton sheets and wooden frames.

INT. SHOP - MORNING

They buy deodorants, a pair of trainers, bandages, a
wrist watch and small individual cartons of orange juice.

EXT. SHOP - MORNING

David waits for the others. Next to him are two police
officers and a WOMAN on her knees. The head officer talks
into a mobile CB Radio. The other is checking the woman's
nails and asks her to show him the soles of her shoes.

                         POLICE OFFICER
                Woman. Brunette. 50 years old. Marital
                Status certificate expired two months ago.

                         WOMAN ARRESTED
                My husband is a lawyer. You're all going to
                be sued.

The police officer with the CB looks to the officer who
was been checking the woman and gives him a nod.

                         POLICE OFFICER
                No dirt under her nails or mud on her
                shoes. 9 Belsize Road.

One of the police officers approaches David.

                         POLICE OFFICER 2
                Good morning, sir. Are you here alone?

                         DAVID
                Good morning, officer. No, I am with my
                partner. She is inside one of the stores
                shopping right now.

                    POLICE OFFICER 2
          Can I see your certificate please?

                    DAVID
          My partner keeps it in her purse. You see,
          I am losing it all the time.

                    POLICE OFFICER 2
          Which is the store she is shopping in, sir?

David tries to remain calm. Shortsighted Woman comes out of the store.

                    SHORTSIGHTED WOMAN
          I'm sorry, darling. They had such a huge
          variety of pain relief creams. I bought
          this one, I think it's the one you were
          looking for.

                    DAVID
          That's wonderful, dear. Can you give me my
          certificate please?

                    SHORTSIGHTED WOMAN
          Of course, darling. Do you want mine also,
          Officer?

Shortsighted Woman kisses him on the cheek.

                    POLICE OFFICER 2
          No, that is alright. You have a nice day,
          sir, madam.

                    DAVID
          You're welcome, Officer.

The officer leaves. Shortsighted Woman hugs David.

EXT. THE CITY - MORNING

Out on the street again. David holds Shortsighted Woman's hand. They don't look at each other, but if anyone took a look at them they'd swear they were a real couple. Loner Leader and Loner Swimmer follow them.

                    DAVID
          If I'm walking too slowly just say and I'll
          up my pace.

                    SHORTSIGHTED WOMAN
          This pace is fine. Maybe don't squeeze my
          hand so tight, my palm's getting a little
          sweaty.

                    DAVID
          Better?

                    SHORTSIGHTED WOMAN
          Yes, much better.

                    DAVID
          Are you planning on buying anything for
          yourself in the city?

                    SHORTSIGHTED WOMAN
          Yes, contact lens solution and a Parker
          Roller ball.

                    DAVID
        I didn't know you were shortsighted. I'm
        shortsighted too.

They stop talking knowingly, as if there's nothing more
to be said.

EXT. APARTMENT BUILDING - DAY

The four loners stand outside the front door of a house.
Loner Leader rings the doorbell. An elderly gentleman
opens the door.

                    LONER LEADER
        Dad?

The gentleman hugs her.

INT. LONER LEADER PARENT'S FLAT - DAY

Loner Leader and her MOTHER talk to a dog on the balcony of the flat, but we can't hear what's being said. The rest sit around a large table and drink orange squash. The couples are very tender with each other. David checks on Loner Leader from time to time. We don't know what connects her to the animal, if it was her brother, sister, uncle or just some normal dog. She comes back to the table and sits down.

                    LONER LEADER'S FATHER
        Will you stay a few days?

                    LONER LEADER
        I'm afraid not, Dad. We're heading back
        again today. Tomorrow I'm going away on a
        business trip. You know how demanding my
        job is – don't ask if I can stay a few days
        every time I come.

                    LONER LEADER'S FATHER
        Do you all work for the same company?

                    DAVID
        Yes.

                    LONER LEADER'S FATHER
        My daughter tells me it's a very fine company. Do you agree?

David struggles to keep things vague but consistent.

                    DAVID
        It's a rather good company, yes. One of the
        best, I'd say. The only problem with the
        job is that I don't have enough time for my
        wife and kids.

                    SHORTSIGHTED WOMAN
        We have four beautiful, healthy children.

                    LONER LEADER'S FATHER
        Congratulations.

                    DAVID
          But even if we'd never had children, I'd
          never dream of leaving my wife. Even
          if it was just the two of us, on our own,
          we'd go on trips, we'd go to Portofino
          in Italy or to a Greek island for the sum-
          mer and so our relationship would be as
          intense as it was at the start. I love her
          so much I could die for her. That's how
          much I love her.

He takes Shortsighted Woman's hand and kisses her on the
lips in front of everyone for quite some time.

EXT. CITY STREET - NIGHT

The two supposed couples walk down the street. David and
Shortsighted Woman walk in perfect sync.

                    LONER LEADER
          Well done. For your first day in the
          city, you did great. That bit about holiday
          destinations in the Mediterranean was
          brilliant.

                    DAVID
          Thank you very much.

They feel proud. Shortsighted Woman tightens her grip on
David's hand.

EXT. THE WOODS - EVENING

David prepares to hunt rabbits. He puts pain relief cream
on his back. He sets up rabbit traps using three wooden
sticks and a big stone. He joins the sticks together
to form the shape of a 4 and then places the stone on
the biggest stick. When the rabbit tries to take the bait
under the rock, the trigger stick moves and the stone
falls on the animal.

                    FEMALE V.O.
          You carefully flay the rabbit with a
          sharp knife and cut off its head. You then
          slice open its belly and stuff it with
          well-washed red and green peppers, not too
          spicy, and a little garlic and mint.

EXT. THE WOODS - END OF DAY

We see that David has caught three rabbits. His hands
are covered in blood from the slaughtered animals.
He puts the dead rabbits in a large sack, dripping with
blood.

                    FEMALE V.O.
          You then soak it in lemon juice and leave
          it a while to marinate the flesh, skewer
          it on a stick and roast it over the fire
          for about an hour. That's my favorite food,
          rabbit.

He leaves two of the rabbits beside the sleeping Shortsighted Woman.

EXT. THE WOODS - MORNING

David sleeps wakes up, gets up and goes to the river's edge to wash his face. As he pulls up his shirt sleeves, he sees a phrase written on his hand in Biro: "River bank, 11 a.m." He rubs the note off with water, looking round to see if anyone is watching.

EXT. RIVER BANK - MORNING

David and Shortsighted Woman sit side by side. It's the first time they are alone together, so they are both a bit tense. At first they avoid making eye contact and talk with long pauses. He is more shy than she is.

> DAVID
> When did you become shortsighted?

> SHORTSIGHTED WOMAN
> When I was 16. You?

> DAVID
> When I was 12.

> SHORTSIGHTED WOMAN
> What make were your first pair of glasses?

> DAVID
> I don't remember.

> SHORTSIGHTED WOMAN
> Do you have astigmatism too?

> DAVID
> Yes.

> SHORTSIGHTED WOMAN
> Would you like me to rub some balm on your back, on the bits you can't reach on your own?

> DAVID
> I'd like that.

Shortsighted Woman takes the jar of Tiger Balm from his bag and rubs it onto his back.

EXT. THE WOODS - EVENING

Loner Leader gives the other loners clothes like the ones worn by the hotel guests, and Loner Swimmer hands out a pistol to Loner Leader. She opens the blue folder the Maid gave her. The loners pay close attention. They are silent and highly disciplined.

> LONER LEADER
> Good evening, everyone, and good luck. I hope you can read my handwriting without any trouble. The room numbers are as follows. Room 306, the Hotel Manager and her Partner, they both have nice voices. Room 240, couple who both love to ski. Room 282, couple who both studied, I'm sorry, I can't quite make it out, couple who both studied... I think it's social sciences. Pier, name of yacht Bliss, couple prone to nosebleeds.

David waits in line. He also takes a set of clothes.

EXT. THE WOODS - NIGHT

The loners walk through the woods with flashlights. They don't talk or, if they do, they whisper.

First in line is Loner Leader. Shortsighted Woman follows and then Loner Swimmer. David is last in line. He looks slightly worried.

EXT. HOTEL GROUNDS - NIGHT

The loners enter the hotel gardens. They check to see if there are any waiter guards around and hide behind some bushes. David goes up to Loner Leader.

> LONER LEADER
> You and you, take 306, you and you take 240, you, you and you take 282, you take the yacht.

David jumps in.

> DAVID
> Can I go to the pier?

> LONER LEADER
> Okay then, you go to the yacht and you go to 282. We'll take the Manager's room. We have 40 minutes.

The loners split up and head off in different directions.

INT. ROOM 306 - NIGHT

Loner Leader, Loner Swimmer and Shortsighted Woman stand over the Hotel Manager and her Partner. The couple look shocked as they lie in their bed. The loners grab the Hotel Manager, tie her to a chair with rope and stuff her mouth with a napkin. Loner Leader speaks to the Hotel Manager's Partner, aiming her gun at him. She takes a look at the note the Maid gave her.

> LONER LEADER
> So, you both have nice voices, is that right?

> HOTEL MANAGER'S PARTNER
> Yes.

> LONER LEADER
> Do you prefer singing duets or when one of you sings the lead and the other does backing vocals?

> HOTEL MANAGER'S PARTNER
> Duets, mostly.

As the dialogue plays out, Shortsighted Woman picks up a pen, a notebook and a couple of CD's and slips them into her bag without anyone noticing. Loner Leader addresses the Hotel Manager's Partner again.

> LONER LEADER
> Do you love her?

                    HOTEL MANAGER'S PARTNER
          With all my heart.

                    LONER LEADER
          How much do you love her, on a scale of one
          to fifteen?

                    HOTEL MANAGER'S PARTNER
          Fourteen.

                    LONER LEADER
          Well, fourteen is a very impressive score.

Loner Leader looks at the Shortsighted Woman.

                    LONER LEADER (CONT'D)
          He loves her very much indeed. Who do you
          think we should kill? Who will be able to
          live on their own better?

                    SHORTSIGHTED WOMAN
          I think we should kill him. If his love for
          her is fourteen out of fifteen then he'll
          most probably commit suicide if she dies or
          else he'll try to find some other partner
          quickly in order to forget her.

                    LONER LEADER
          I'm not so sure. I have to think about
          this.

Loner Leader thinks hard before addressing the Hotel
Manager's Partner once more.

                    LONER LEADER (CONT'D)
          You, if this woman dies, do you think
          you'll manage on your own or will you get
          involved with someone else?

                    HOTEL MANAGER'S PARTNER
          No. I can live alone, but she can't. I'm
          on my own for hours while she's running the
          hotel. I like sitting in the room, it re-
          laxes me, calms me, I like it a lot. I can
          definitely live on my own.

Loner Leader hands the Hotel Manager's Partner the pistol. He seems startled at first. Then he looks the
Hotel Manager straight in the eye and mercilessly pulls
the trigger. The gun doesn't fire. It isn't loaded. The
three loners leave them alone together.

EXT. HOTEL GROUNDS - NIGHT

David walks quickly. He holds a tranquilliser gun.
He goes towards the pier.

EXT. PIER - NIGHT

Two waiters guard the pier. Automatic rifles are slung
across their backs. But they seem relaxed and not very
alert. The light is on in one of the three yachts.

                    GUARD WAITER 1
          The only thing that troubles me is when
          someone orders something and then they in-
          sist they ordered something else. For exam-
          ple, someone says they want an espresso and
          then say they didn't order an espresso but
          a cappuccino, and get all rude about it and
          annoyed. I find that quite troubling.

                    GUARD WAITER 2
          In situations like that you need to be
          polite and make them realise their mistake.
          If this gets you nowhere, then take back
          their espresso and bring them a cappuccino
          — that way you avoid any hassle. If the
          problem doesn't go away, if they use physi-
          cal violence, or if they continue to change
          what they asked you for, you just have to
          speak with the Manager. Understood?

                    GUARD WAITER 1
          Yes.

David swiftly shoots them both from a distance with his
tranquilliser gun. They fall down unconscious. He climbs
down a ladder attached to the pier and gets into a small
boat. He paddles towards the yachts.

INT. YACHT - NIGHT

David climbs aboard the yacht. He carefully looks through
the cabin window.

Limping Man and Nosebleed Woman wear identical nautical
striped outfits. His is stained with blood. Their child,
Elizabeth, also sits with them.

                    LIMPING MAN
          A basketball weighs between 550 and 650
          grams. Did you know that?

                    NOSEBLEED WOMAN
          No, I didn't know that.

                    LIMPING MAN
          Yes. Its weight is different for men's and
          women's games, but that's roughly how much
          they weigh. Do you know how much a volley-
          ball weighs?

                    ELIZABETH
          No, but I'd love to find out.

David startles them, appearing behind the little girl.
He sits down beside them at the table and places the gun
next to him.

                    DAVID
          Good evening. His nose doesn't really bleed
          on its own. He bangs it against a wall or
          a piece of wood or some other hard surface,
          or else he cuts it with a pen knife while
          you aren't looking. You two are not suited.

                    ELIZABETH
          Shut up. Dad, tell him to leave.
          I'm sleepy.

                    DAVID
          I'm sure that the stain on his t-shirt is
          not blood but cherry juice or tomato
          ketchup or red watercolour paint or some-
          thing like that.

Nosebleed Woman slaps David in the face.

                    DAVID (CONT'D)
          Or beetroot juice.

Elizabeth grabs the knife from the table.

                    ELIZABETH
          Kill him. Mum, here's the knife. Kill him.

Limping Man pushes David out of the cabin.

                    LIMPING MAN
          Get out of here while you still can.

David looks at them with a weird mix of shame and contempt and then leaves.

EXT. PIER - NIGHT

David returns to the pier and starts to run towards
a spot where the other loners are waiting for him. Shortsighted Woman smiles slightly the moment she sees him
returning safe. The Maid follows the loners as they dis-
appear into the woods. She is finally part of them.

EXT. THE WOODS - AFTERNOON

The loners dance, everyone on their own, wearing headsets. The Maid dances impressively well. A few feet away,
with his back turned to her, Loner Swimmer dances also,
but not so gracefully. David does not dance at all.
He tries to find Shortsighted Woman amongst the others.
He sees her but before he has time to approach her, Loner
Leader goes up to David.

                    LONER LEADER
          Where were you? I was looking for you.

                    DAVID
          I was masturbating behind those bushes.

                    LONER LEADER
          Why aren't you dancing?

                    DAVID
          My leg hurts a little.

                    LONER LEADER
          Did you dig your own grave?

                    DAVID
          Not yet.

                    LONER LEADER
          I don't mean to pressure you, or to ruin
          the mood now that we're celebrating, but
          at some point you'll have to do it. Don't
          expect anyone else to dig your grave for
          you, or to carry your corpse. We'll throw
          some dirt over you but that's about it.

Tomorrow find a spot you like where the
ground isn't too rocky and make a start.
Enjoy the rest of your evening.

EXT. THE WOODS - DAY

David sees Loner Swimmer taking rabbits to Shortsighted
Woman. She smiles and says something to him, he then
says something back. It must have been something very
funny because he laughs loudly then waves her goodbye and
leaves. As soon as Loner Swimmer is gone, David goes up
to her. He's obviously upset but tries to hide it.

DAVID
Did you catch rabbits?

SHORTSIGHTED WOMAN
No, someone brought me them.

DAVID
Who?

SHORTSIGHTED WOMAN
A friend of mine. You want one?

DAVID
No.

SHORTSIGHTED WOMAN
You're jealous?

DAVID
No, I'm not jealous. It's just you don't
need to accept rabbits from other people.
If you need more rabbits, just tell me and
I'll bring you more. Catching a rabbit is
difficult, but I'll try harder. There's no
need for you to be indebted to the others.

SHORTSIGHTED WOMAN
Thank you very much.

DAVID
That man who brought you the rabbits, is he
shortsighted?

SHORTSIGHTED WOMAN
I don't know. I don't think so.

EXT. THE WOODS - DAY

David goes up to Loner Swimmer, who's shaving his
face in the river. He stares at him for a while, then
speaks loudly.

DAVID
Is that a sparrow up in that tree?

LONER SWIMMER
I can't really see that far, but I don't
think so.

DAVID
Are you shortsighted?

LONER SWIMMER
No.

                    DAVID
          You're lying.

                    LONER SWIMMER
          It's the truth.

                    DAVID
          What does it say here?

David shows him the zip on his jacket.

                    LONER SWIMMER
          YKK.

                    DAVID
          You knew that already. All zips say the
          same thing.

                    LONER SWIMMER
          I'm not shortsighted. I don't understand
          why you won't believe me. I can see very
          clearly. I used to be a pilot.

                    DAVID
          You're wearing contact lenses.

                    LONER SWIMMER
          I'm not wearing contact lenses. I'm not
          shortsighted, I swear.

                    DAVID
          You are. You think I'm an idiot and can't
          tell.

David hits him, kicks him and pins him down. He pulls open his eyelids.

                    DAVID (CONT'D)
          Look up. I said, look up.

Loner Swimmer obeys. David fingers his eyeballs to check whether he's wearing contact lenses or not.

                    DAVID (CONT'D)
          Now down. Left and right.

David gets up. Loner Swimmer stays down on the ground.

                    DAVID (CONT'D)
          I'm sorry. I thought you were trying to
          fool me. I'm sorry.

EXT. THE WOODS - DAY

David and Shortsighted Woman hold their CD players. Beside them stands a pony; it might be that girl from the hotel.

                    DAVID
          For this synchronization exercise we need
          to fully concentrate as we both have to
          press play at the same time. I'll count
          down from five and we'll push the button on
          zero.

                    SHORTSIGHTED WOMAN
          Why don't we use only one headset?

> DAVID
> Because that's the whole point. It's an exercise for us. We have to be totally synchronised.

> SHORTSIGHTED WOMAN
> Ok. I'm ready.

> DAVID
> Five, four, three, two, one, zero.

The both push their buttons and dance in each other's arms. We hear the same song playing twice, overlaid, the two streams a little out of sync. As they dance, they kiss each other.

EXT. THE WOODS - MORNING

During the voiceover, we see various scenes from the lives of the loners. Loner Swimmer and other loners watch a dog attacking a seal in the middle of the woods.

> FEMALE V.O.
> We've developed a code so that we can communicate with each other, even in front of the others, without them knowing what we are saying.

EXT. THE WOODS - NIGHT

A loner fighting with another loner.

> FEMALE V.O.
> When we turn our heads to the left it means "I love you more than anything in the world" and when we turn our heads to the right it means "Watch out, we're in danger." We had to be very careful in the beginning not to mix up "I love you more than anything in the world" with "Watch out, we're in danger." When we raise our left arm it means "I want to dance in your arms."

EXT. THE WOODS - DAY

A loner lying dead, loners washing themselves in the river, Loner Leader feeding the pig.

> FEMALE V.O.
> A handstand means "I miss you so much." When we make a fist and put it behind our backs it means "Let's fuck, I'm horny." The code grew more and more as time went by and within a few weeks we could talk about almost anything without even opening our mouths. About history, music, architecture, everything.

INT. LONER LEADER'S PARENTS' FLAT - MORNING

Loner Leader, Loner Swimmer, her father, and her mother sit on the sofa. They all seem relaxed; they've been drinking and they're enjoying the stories told by the elderly couple. David and Shortsighted Woman sit in a corner.

                    LONER LEADER'S FATHER
          I met her mother at school. We were both
          top of the class in music. I was a little
          better than her because my fingers are
          longer and stronger, which is very import-
          ant when playing the guitar. She was bet-
          ter at singing. We began meeting to study
          together. We became a couple just a month
          before leaving school. If we'd waited
          one more month, we'd have been sent to the
          hotel. Can you imagine?

                    LONER SWIMMER
          Let's not talk about unpleasant things.
          I can't wait for you both to play us
          some music.

Loner Leader's father and mother begin to play a duo
on their guitars very skillfully. David kisses Shortsighted Woman on the hand. She begins to stroke his
hair and then French kisses him for a long time. Loner
Leader, annoyed, slaps them.

                    LONER LEADER
          That's enough. Show my parents some
          respect, they're playing you music.

                    LONER LEADER'S MOTHER
          That's okay.

                    LONER LEADER
          No mother, it is not okay. Please,
          continue.

                    LONER LEADER'S MOTHER
          Do you want us to perform the same song,
          or something else?

                    LONER LEADER
          Something else.

EXT. CITY STREET - MORNING

Loner Leader and Loner Swimmer go on ahead. David and
Shortsighted Woman follow behind. They regret being
so intimate at the gathering. David tries to read Loner
Leader, to figure out if she suspects them or not.

                    DAVID
          We were great today, weren't we? Maybe even
          better than last time.

Loner Leader says nothing. They walk quickly.

                    DAVID (CONT'D)
          Didn't her parents sing and play
          beautifully?

                    SHORTSIGHTED WOMAN
          It was wonderful.

David and Shortsighted Woman smile but seem worried.

EXT. THE WOODS - MORNING

The loners eat fruit together. Loner Leader hands out bananas. They sit around a tree trunk. David covers his left eye with his hand.

Shortsighted Woman makes a fist and puts it behind her back. All part of their secret code that nobody else understands. Loner Swimmer smiles without really understanding what's going on. A pink flamingo stands in the distance.

EXT. THE WOODS - EVENING

The Maid reads from a notebook. Her voice is that of the Female V.O. we've been hearing throughout the story. Loner Leader listens beside her.

> MAID (FEMALE V.O.)
> "We love each other and we suit each other. That's the reason why we've decided to leave and stay together forever in the city. Tomorrow, during the hunt, we're going to disappear and everyone will think we've been captured and that we're going to be turned into dogs or canaries or something. I think the first thing I'm going to do when I get into the city is buy a bathrobe and then we'll go to a pool with a high diving board perfect for diving. And we'll do lots of different things together, serious things not silly ones, like go for walks in the park or play the guitar together." That's where it ends. There are some notes at the back but I don't think they're important.

Loner Leader stands perfectly still. She seems shocked and enraged even though she kind of suspected it.

> LONER LEADER
> Read me the notes.

> MAID
> "Portofino: Italian fishing village and upmarket resort famous for its picturesque harbour. Population: 439. Beaches nearby: Paraggi Beach, Camogli, Chiavari and Lavagna. Serifos: Greek island located in the western Cyclades. Population: 1,414. The Miners' Strike of 1916. In the 20th century, the mines of Serifos were exploited by the mining company "Société Minière Sérifos-Spiliazeza" under the direction of the German mineralogist A. Grohmann, who died in 1905."

> LONER LEADER
> That's enough. Where did you find it?

> MAID
> In the woods. Someone probably dropped it during the hunt.

> LONER LEADER
> Give it to me. I'll deal with it.

She takes the notebook and leaves.

EXT. THE WOODS - EVENING

Loner Leader goes up to Shortsighted Woman. She's reading a book by torchlight. Loner Leader sits next to her and talks to her in a really friendly tone of voice.

LONER LEADER
You're reading?

SHORTSIGHTED WOMAN
Yes.

LONER LEADER
Wouldn't it be amazing if you could read without the help of glasses or contacts?

SHORTSIGHTED WOMAN
Yes.

LONER LEADER
I'd like to ask you a favour.

SHORTSIGHTED WOMAN
What sort of favour?

LONER LEADER
Do you have a sheet of white paper, by any chance? I want to make a list of the stuff we need from the city and there's no paper left in my notebook.

Shortsighted Woman looks in her backpack for her notebook. She starts rummaging, distressed.

LONER LEADER (CONT'D)
It's fine if you don't have any. I'll ask someone else.

SHORTSIGHTED WOMAN
But I do. I'm sure I have a notebook with white pages, it's in here somewhere, I'm sure of it.

LONER LEADER
Don't worry. It doesn't matter. I'll make a note to buy you a new one.

Loner Leader tenderly touches Shortsighted Woman on her shoulder and leaves.

INT. DOCTOR'S SURGERY WAITING ROOM - MORNING

Loner Leader, the Maid and Shortsighted Woman are in a waiting room. The three women are seated on a sofa. There is a coffee table with past issues of various magazines in front of them. The Maid reads one of these magazines. Shortsighted Woman stands up.

SHORTSIGHTED WOMAN
I think we should leave right now. The three of us coming here and not four or two is very dangerous. How didn't we think of that earlier? It's highly likely the doctor will suspect us. I suggest we leave the first chance we get. Right now, in fact.

                    LONER LEADER
         Don't be afraid. No one will suspect
         a thing. I bet you weren't expecting this
         surprise. Isn't it wonderful?

                    SHORTSIGHTED WOMAN
         Yes, it is. Still, I'd like to think it
         over for a few days, and maybe I'll
         have the surgery done when we're next in
         the city.

                    LONER LEADER
         What's there to think about? If it's better
         to see clearly or to be shortsighted, is
         that it? That's absurd, you know that. Any-
         way, this doctor is the best there is, it's
         really very difficult to get an appoint-
         ment. I called him months ago to get him to
         see you today.

A SECRETARY goes up to them and shows them the door to
the doctor's office.

INT. DOCTOR'S OFFICE - MORNING

The DOCTOR sits behind his desk. Loner Leader and Shortsighted Woman sit in two chairs opposite him. This is
a typical doctor's office: big wooden bookcase, a mix
of old-fashioned and modern furniture, some framed prints
of famous paintings. The doctor's hands are shiny and
clean, like the hands of most doctors.

                    DOCTOR
         This operation is what we call "routine
         surgery." It has a 90% success rate, so
         there's no need to worry. There are no
         scalpels involved; the entire procedure is
         done by laser. There's no reason why you
         shouldn't see clearly when you're swimming
         in the sea or when you first wake up in
         the morning. Contact lens solution, contact
         lens cases, eyeglasses, all that will be
         a thing of the past.

                    LONER LEADER
         Thank you very much, doctor.

Shortsighted woman doesn't speak. She makes quite an
effort to appear happy but doesn't make a very good job
of it.

INT. OPERATING THEATRE - MORNING

Shortsighted Woman lies frightened on an operating table.
She looks around, sweating. The Doctor sedates her by
an intravenous injection. He then lays out various scalpels on a metal tray.

INT. DOCTOR'S SURGERY WAITING ROOM - DAY

Loner Leader sits and waits. The Doctor brings out Shortsighted Woman, whose eyes are bandaged up. The Maid approaches Shortsighted Woman and gives her a hug. She then
puts her jacket over Shortsighted Woman's shoulders and
fixes her hair with her hands. Loner Leader pays the
Doctor. He has a quiet word with Loner Leader but we cannot hear what he says very clearly.

                    DOCTOR (whispers)
          She is blind.

                    LONER LEADER
          Thank you.

EXT. THE WOODS - DAY

Shortsighted Woman, kneeling on the ground, holds
a knife. It looks like there's just been a fight.
She's flushed red. Unable to see, her eyes still
bandaged up, Shortsighted Woman threatens anyone who
might be close to her with her knife. Loner Leader
and the Maid keep their distance.

                    LONER LEADER
          Throw down your knife and stand up.

                    SHORTSIGHTED WOMAN
          No.

                    LONER LEADER
          You're being completely irrational. I
          understand you're upset by the unexpected
          results but to accuse me is very insult-
          ing to say the least. The doctor said there
          were some unforeseen complications after
          your surgery. That is all. Who would
          have guessed such a simple procedure could
          have such catastrophic results? No one.
          Anyway, what reason could I possibly have
          had to do such a hideous thing on purpose?

                    SHORTSIGHTED WOMAN
          Why did you have to blind me? You could
          have blinded him.

                    LONER LEADER
          I have no idea what you're talking about.
          The drugs are messing with your head. If
          I were you, I'd try and be a little braver
          about the whole thing. Now get up and give
          me the knife, or I'll hit you and take it
          by force.

Shortsighted Woman says nothing. She's still holding the
knife in a threatening manner.

                    LONER LEADER (CONT'D)
          Here I come.

Loner Leader signals to the Maid, who goes over to Shortsighted Woman. She grabs the hand holding the knife and
they begin to fight. Loner Leader speaks close to the
Maid's head, so that the Shortsighted Woman, who is now
blind, thinks she's wrestling with Loner Leader.

                    SHORTSIGHTED WOMAN
          I swear I'm going to kill you.

                    LONER LEADER
          No, don't, please. Let go of my hair,
          you're hurting me.

Shortsighted Woman has grabbed the Maid by the hair and now stabs her in the stomach. Loner Leader stays close so that it seems it's really her fighting Shortsighted Woman and groans in pain with each stab.

> LONER LEADER (CONT'D)
> Have mercy, please, [groans] don't kill me. Just think [groans] that when someone [groans] goes blind, one of their other senses [groans] is heightened. Touch, hearing, smell [groans]. You'll smell better, hear better. You'll feel things with your fingers and know what it is you're touching [groans].

Silence. The Maid has been dead some time now. Shortsighted Woman raises herself up a little. She feels out the dead woman's body with her hands and takes her pulse. She puts down the bloody knife, wipes her hands and gets up. That is when Loner Leader begins her monologue again. Shortsighted Woman jumps in fear.

> LONER LEADER (CONT'D)
> You could also catch a dog in the woods and train it to guide you. Dogs can do that, you know. I'll help you catch a dog myself. Now that I think of it, your sense of touch may already be heightened. Let's find out right now. I'll put something in your hand and you tell me what it is. Okay?

Loner Leader gives her something and closes her hand around it tight.

> LONER LEADER (CONT'D)
> Make a fist. Feel what it is, feel its shape. It's not difficult.

Shortsighted Woman falls down and screams. Loner Leader continues to squeeze her fist.

> LONER LEADER (CONT'D)
> What is it? What is it? I'll give you a little more time to guess but I can't wait much longer. What is it?

Shortsighted Woman screams. Loner Leader lets go of her hand. She opens her fist and her palm is covered in blood.

> LONER LEADER (CONT'D)
> Time's up. It's a small razor blade. It seems your sense of touch hasn't improved yet but it'll happen, you'll see. Now get up. If you carry on acting like this I'm going to leave you here and I don't think you'll manage to find meeting point two on your own.

EXT. THE WOODS - DAY

David meets with Shortsighted Woman. She sits on a rock. She has taken the bandages off and wears sunglasses. She tries to act calm.

> DAVID
> Did you have a nice time in the city?

                    SHORTSIGHTED WOMAN
          Sure.

                    DAVID
          What happened to your hand?

                    SHORTSIGHTED WOMAN
          I was cutting a tree branch with a knife,
          and cut myself by accident. You look
          handsome today. Did you get your hair cut?

                    DAVID
          Thank you. No, I didn't get a haircut, I'm
          going to have my hair cut today. Look what
          I brought you.

                    SHORTSIGHTED WOMAN
          Thank you very much. I'm so hungry, I'll
          eat it right away.

David is momentarily puzzled.

                    DAVID
          It's a bigger flashlight.

                    SHORTSIGHTED WOMAN
          I'm sorry, it's so big I thought it was a
          rabbit. It's the biggest flashlight I've
          ever seen.
                    DAVID
          Are you ready for tonight?

Shortsighted Woman decides to drop her act.

                    SHORTSIGHTED WOMAN
          Of course I am. I want to tell you some-
          thing but please don't get angry.

                    DAVID
          What happened?

                    SHORTSIGHTED WOMAN
          I can't see a thing. I'm blind.

                    DAVID
          What do you mean?

                    SHORTSIGHTED WOMAN
          There's no point lying to you, you'll find
          out sooner or later. I've lost my sight.
          Loner Leader blinded me this morning, in
          the city. She must have realised that I
          love you and you love me and that we were
          going to leave for the city.

                    DAVID
          How did she find out?

                    SHORTSIGHTED WOMAN
          I don't know. I think she found my note-
          book.

                    DAVID
          What notebook?

                    SHORTSIGHTED WOMAN
          My notebook. I had a notebook, where I'd
          write my thoughts about us, about how suit-
          ed we are. I'm sorry.

                    DAVID
          You can't see at all?

                    SHORTSIGHTED WOMAN
          No, not at all.

                    DAVID
          And when you asked if I'd had a haircut?

                    SHORTSIGHTED WOMAN
          I said it so you wouldn't realise I can't
          see. I'm sorry.

David kicks some dirt. He seems frustrated and disappointed. He turns towards Shortsighted Woman.

                    DAVID
          Don't cry. Crying will make your eyes hurt
          even more. We'll find a way.

EXT. THE WOODS - NIGHT

Some loners sleep, others listen to music with their
headsets. David lies on the ground and seems very
sad. Loner Leader goes up to David, holding a pig on
a leash.

                    LONER LEADER
          I'm going to hunt for truffles. Do you want
          to come and keep me company?

                    DAVID
          I'm a little sleepy.

                    LONER LEADER
          We won't be long. I've found a spot where
          there are lots of them. We won't be long, I
          promise. Come on.

David gets up.

EXT. THE WOODS - NIGHT

David and Loner Leader walk through the woods holding
flashlights. David looks scared. He doesn't know if he's
about to be punished as well.

                    LONER LEADER
          Thanks for coming with me. Something
          terrible happened today and I needed some
          company.

                    DAVID
          What happened?

                    LONER LEADER
          Didn't you hear what happened in the city?

                    DAVID
          No.

LONER LEADER
Emma had an operation and went blind. It's so very sad. And then my new deputy leader was killed on our way back. She was attacked by a jaguar. I'm really very upset because I was thinking of making Emma deputy leader as she's very capable and loyal. But then I gave it some thought and realised that now it will be difficult for her to command so many people. The next person I thought could take on such a responsibility is you.

DAVID
Thank you very much.

LONER LEADER
Don't thank me. I trust you completely and I consider you one of the best loners I've seen in years. I know you won't disappoint me in any way. If something happens to me, you will take over. Take a few days to think about it and let me know when you're ready. Here's the place with the truffles. You can't imagine how many there are. I wanted you to come with me and see it for yourself. If you become deputy leader, you'll need to know where in the woods you can find lots of truffles.

EXT. RIVER BANK - MORNING

Shortsighted Woman lies under a tree. David stands beside her holding four carrots and a fish. Apparently he's decided not to give up yet.

DAVID
What blood type are you?

SHORTSIGHTED WOMAN
B.

David thinks some more.

DAVID
Do you like berries? Blueberries? Blackberries?

SHORTSIGHTED WOMAN
No, no.

DAVID
Can you play the piano?

SHORTSIGHTED WOMAN
No.

DAVID
Do you speak German?

SHORTSIGHTED WOMAN
No.

                    DAVID
          I could teach you German but it would take
          at least a year for you to be able to speak
          the basics, not fluently. So there's no
          point. You know, German is one of the most
          difficult languages in the world to learn
          because its grammar is very complicated.

EXT. THE WOODS - MORNING

David sings a duet written for a man and a woman all on
his own. He only sings the male part and leaves out
the female part. A rabbit comes up close to him. David
looks at it but does not kill it. He has no reason to
hunt rabbits anymore. The rabbit hops off.

EXT. RIVER BANK - MORNING

David hands Shortsighted Woman a plastic cup. She feels
it with her fingers.

                    SHORTSIGHTED WOMAN
          A plastic cup.

                    DAVID
          That's right. Very good.

He then hands her a tennis ball.

                    SHORTSIGHTED WOMAN
          A kiwi.

                    DAVID
          That's right. Ten out of ten, again.

She smiles.

                    DAVID
          Can I give you a kiss?

Shortsighted Woman now becomes serious.

                    SHORTSIGHTED WOMAN
          I can't thank you enough for keeping me
          company, for the games and activities, but
          you know we can't do that any more. Do
          you want to play another round of "touch-
          think-guess-win"?

                    DAVID
          No, that's enough for today. In any case,
          I've run out of things to test you
          with. Maybe tomorrow, or one of these days.

                    SHORTSIGHTED WOMAN
          Tomorrow morning?

                    DAVID
          We'll see.

EXT. THE WOODS - DAY

David walks through the woods with Loner Leader. He stops
at some point and looks around.

                    LONER LEADER
          How do you like this place here?

                    DAVID
          It's nice.

                    LONER LEADER
          It is nice, and more importantly very quiet
          because of the rocks you have to climb to
          get here. Can you imagine why I brought you
          to such a quiet place today?

                    DAVID
          No.

                    LONER LEADER
          Because I think it's the perfect spot for
          your grave. It was my second choice for
          my own grave, but in the end I decided on a
          place a little to the north of here because
          there are fewer dogs around there, digging
          all the time for bones.

She takes a small pickaxe from her pocket and gives it
to him. David starts to dig. After a while he gets tired
and stops. He's only managed to dig a small hole. He
climbs into it but his whole body won't fit. He tries
to fit as best he can.

                    LONER LEADER (CONT'D)
          You have to make it bigger so you'll fit
          better. As I said, there are a lot of dogs
          around here. Now cover yourself with soil.
          Use your hands.

He scoops some soil onto his body and sits there a
little, motionless.

                    LONER LEADER (CONT'D)
          Over your face too. You wouldn't want your
          face to get eaten, would you?

David puts more soil over his face and body. He seems
terrified.

                    LONER LEADER (CONT'D)
          Can you see how great this spot is?

                    DAVID
          Yes. Thank you very much.

Loner Leader cuts a flower and puts it on David's grave.

                    LONER LEADER
          If you die before me, I'll visit you as
          often I can. I promise.

David stays motionless.

EXT. WOODS - EVENING

David walks in the forest and comes across a pony. The
animal is probably the woman with the nice hair at
the hotel, Nosebleed Woman's Best Friend. David stares
at the pony with a mixture of confusion and anger. His
face is still full of dirt.

                    DAVID
          Hi, how are you? It's very nice meeting
          you again.

He cuts the pony's mane with a pair of scissors. The
animal stands still. He then looks the pony in the eye
and hits it across the face.

>   DAVID (CONT'D)
>   How do you like my hair now?

EXT. THE WOODS - MORNING

Shortsighted Woman and the 2 Bandaged Loners are down
on their knees trying to set a rabbit trap. David
approaches them.

>   DAVID
>   Good afternoon.

>   SHORTSIGHTED WOMAN
>   How are you?

>   DAVID
>   Fine.

>   SHORTSIGHTED WOMAN
>   I'm hungry. You haven't brought me a
>   rabbit in days. Or things for me to touch
>   and guess.

>   DAVID
>   I've got good news. I've had a great idea.
>   Have you got a minute?

>   SHORTSIGHTED WOMAN
>   What sort of idea?

David takes Shortsighted Woman aside and describes
his idea to her using the physical code they've
developed between them, but now describing the movements to her orally.

>   DAVID
>   I raise my left foot. I bring my elbow
>   to my knee and tap it twice. I bring
>   my foot to my knee and tap it three times.
>   I lie face down. I kneel down. I touch
>   my left cheek and then lie face up.

Shortsighted Woman thinks for a minute.

>   SHORTSIGHTED WOMAN
>   Are you sure you are prepared to do that?

>   DAVID
>   It's the only way.

She doesn't speak.

>   DAVID (CONT'D)
>   Yes, of course I am. I wouldn't propose it
>   if I wasn't.

David leaves. Shortsighted Woman smiles but seems unsure
at the same time.

EXT. THE WOODS - NIGHT

David attacks a woman in the dark. He hits her. She falls unconscious and we see the face of Loner Leader. He takes a roll of gaffer tape from his pocket, ties her up and gags her mouth. He then drags her away.

EXT. THE WOODS - NIGHT

Loner Leader, tied up, lies in David's freshly dug grave. Dogs circle the shallow pit. Loner Leader tries in vain to cut herself loose.

EXT. THE WOODS - MORNING

David and Shortsighted Woman walk quickly, as if running with very small steps. David walks a little ahead, and Shortsighted Woman holds his hand and follows behind. They are wearing their civilian clothes but David's suit doesn't fit him very well. It's a little tight. They talk as they walk.

                    DAVID
          Are you thirsty?

                    SHORTSIGHTED WOMAN
          No.

                    DAVID
          It's not much farther. I can already see
          the buildings.

There are no buildings in sight yet.

                    SHORTSIGHTED WOMAN
          That's perfect.

Shortsighted Woman continues to walk, a little faster now.

                    SHORTSIGHTED WOMAN (CONT'D)
          We should speed up a little bit.

                    DAVID
          These trousers are too tight. I'm sorry.
          It was dark and I couldn't see clearly
          and I didn't have the time to try them on.
          I'm sorry.

                    SHORTSIGHTED WOMAN
          Never mind.

EXT. MAIN ROAD - MIDDAY

David and Shortsighted Woman come out of the woods and onto the road. They walk more slowly now. David hears a noise. He turns and sees a vehicle coming in the distance. He pulls Shortsighted Woman off the road and they hide in some bushes. The vehicle passes them. It is the hotel coach heading into town.

                    DAVID
          It's gone. They didn't see us.

                    SHORTSIGHTED WOMAN
          I'm a little hungry. If you see a rabbit,
          kill it and we'll eat.

                        DAVID
        We don't have time to hunt. We'll eat when
        we get into the city. Everything has to
        happen as we said, without delay, without
        wasting time for no reason. We have
        to reach the restaurant before rush hour.
        It'll be much easier if there aren't lots
        of people coming and going in the toilets.

                        SHORTSIGHTED WOMAN
        Have you decided how you're going to do it?

                        DAVID
        No.

                        SHORTSIGHTED WOMAN
        Alright. Let's not waste any more time
        talking. Let's go.

They get up and head off again down the road.

IV. THE CITY

INT. CITY RESTAURANT - DAY

David and Shortsighted Woman sit at a table. There aren't many people in the restaurant, just another couple sitting a few tables further back. In front of them are two glasses of water. They are silent.

                        DAVID
        Profile.

Shortsighted Woman turns her head to the left, holds it there, then turns it to the right and holds it there.

                        DAVID (CONT'D)
        Fingers.

Shortsighted Woman shows him her fingers. David looks at them carefully.

                        DAVID (CONT'D)
        Elbows.

Shortsighted Woman pulls up her sleeves and shows him her elbows.

                        SHORTSIGHTED WOMAN
        Would you like me to show you my belly?

                        DAVID
        No, I remember your belly very well.
        Smile.

Shortsighted Woman smiles. She holds the smile for a long time. David signals to a RESTAURANT WAITER. The waiter comes to their table.

                        DAVID (CONT'D)
        Can I have a knife and fork, please? Not a
        butter knife. A steak knife.

                        RESTAURANT WAITER
        Certainly.

The waiter brings him a knife and fork wrapped in a napkin. David examines both pieces of cutlery. He takes the knife and wraps the fork back up in the napkin.

>   DAVID
> I'm going to do it with a knife.

>   SHORTSIGHTED WOMAN
> Do you want me to come with you?

>   DAVID
> I'd rather you didn't.

>   SHORTSIGHTED WOMAN
> Don't worry. It's strange at first but
> you get used to it. And your other
> senses are heightened. Touch, for example.
> Your hearing.

>   DAVID
> I know.

David gets up from his chair. He heads towards the toilets.

INT. CITY RESTAURANT TOILETS - DAY

David pulls lots of paper towels out of the dispenser. He tucks them into his shirt collar and lays them over his shoulders to keep the blood off. He looks at himself in the mirror, checks to see if his hands are trembling and then raises the knife, bringing it close to his eye. Closer and closer. He can't do it, and lowers the knife again. He then takes a few deep breaths and tries again.

INT. CITY RESTAURANT - DAY

Shortsighted Woman sits on her own at the table and waits. The waiter fills her glass with water and leaves. We hear many different voices and a door opening and closing. A couple sits down at the table next to her. Shortsighted Woman takes a small sip of water and puts her glass back down on the table. Beside her is the restaurant front window, which looks onto a main road. Cars go by. Various couples walk past, some of them have kids, others a dog. The scene lasts some time.

>   THE END.

>   FEMALE V.O.
>   (EXTRA, TO BE RECORDED AS WILD TRACK)
> 1. There were times he was thinking a
> million things simultaneously. The even-
> tuality of shaving his mustache, that he
> wanted to smoke a cigarette, his sister
> skiing, the advantages of a multi-story
> house, Bob, women's hair, the lyrics of a
> particular song, the spelling of a partic-
> ular word, and a well done piece of meat,
> for example. All at the same time.
>
> 2. He is the sun, he is the woods, the
> food, the leaves of the palm trees, the
> milk of the cows, he is my dear. My dear.
> He is the armchair and the leather slip-
> pers, he is the swimming pool in the
> middle of a neat garden, he is the night,
> he is the shaved cheek I kiss. My dear.

SECTION

II

SECTION II

24 FRAMES

Cinematography by Thimios Bakatakis

THE LOBSTER

00:06:28
00:08:41
00:14:00
00:17:10
00:20:55
00:24:30
00:26:47
00:33:55
00:35:48
00:38:00
00:45:47
00:55:07
00:59:58
01:10:20
01:17:36
01:25:56
01:26:54
01:30:04
01:31:10
01:39:27
01:43:03
01:48:53
01:51:49
01:53:36

92

00:06:28

93

94

00:08:41

95

96

00:14:00

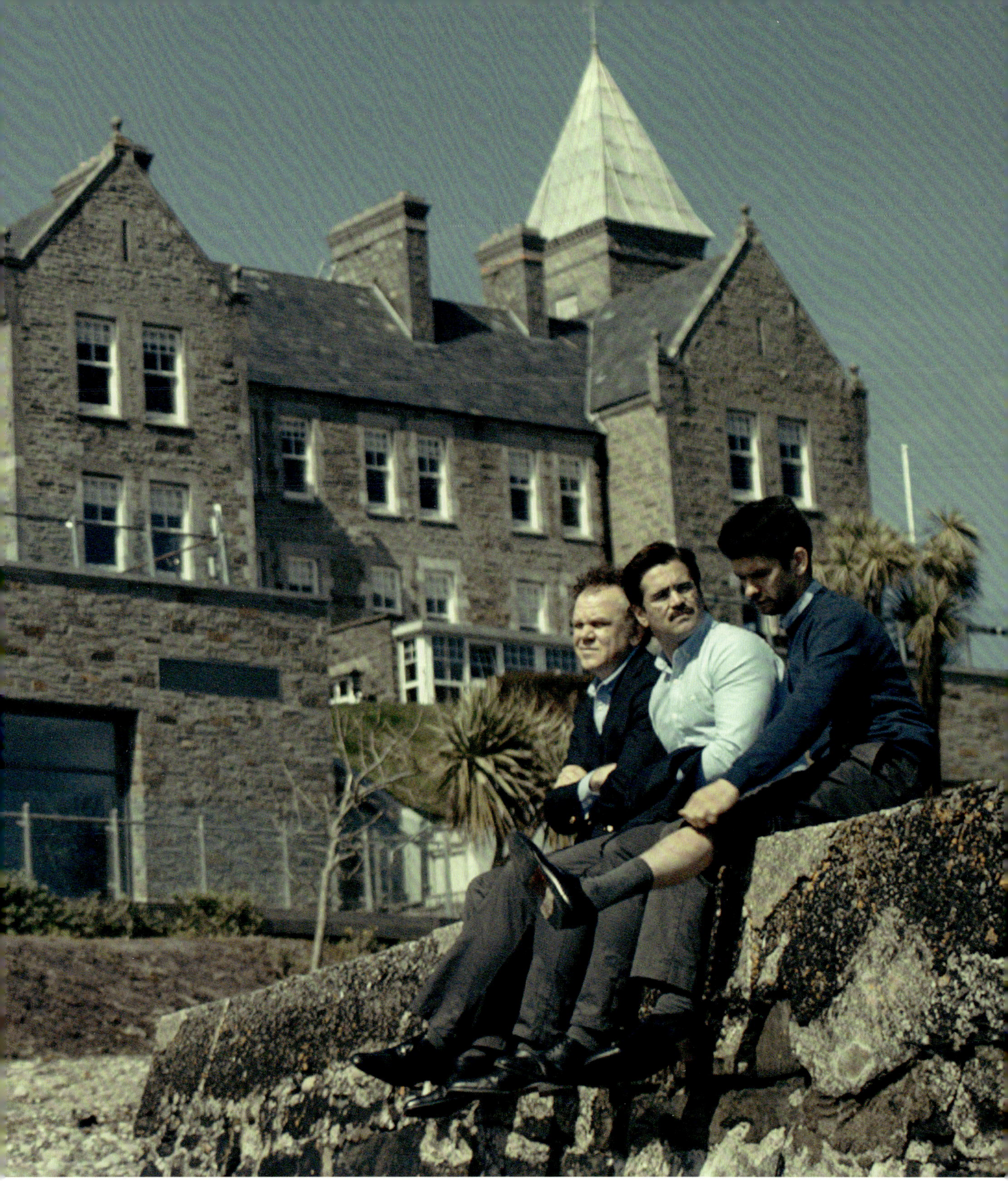

98

00:17:10

99

100

101

102

00:24:30

103

104

00:26:47

105

106

00:33:55

107

108

00:35:48

109

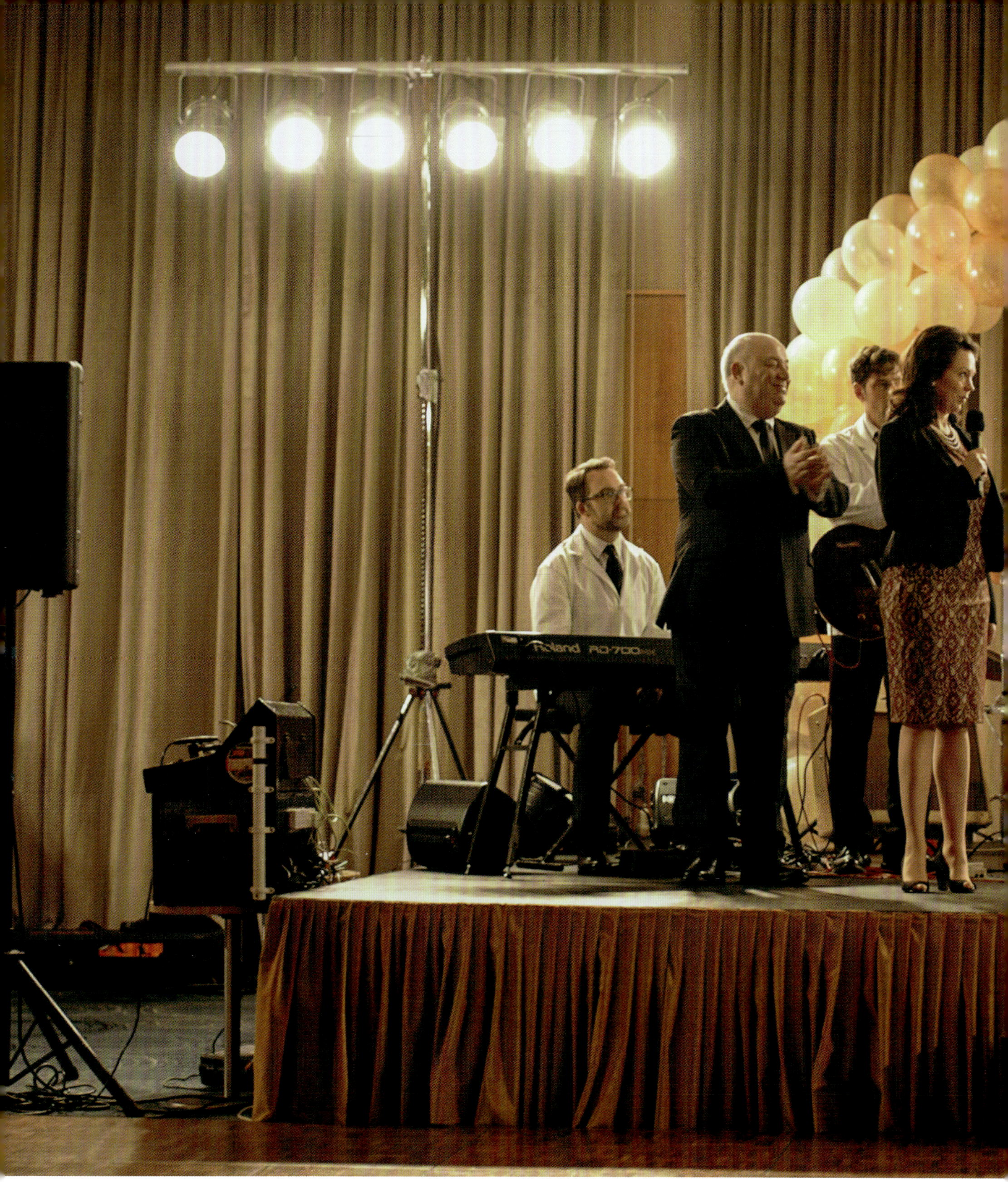

110

00:38:00

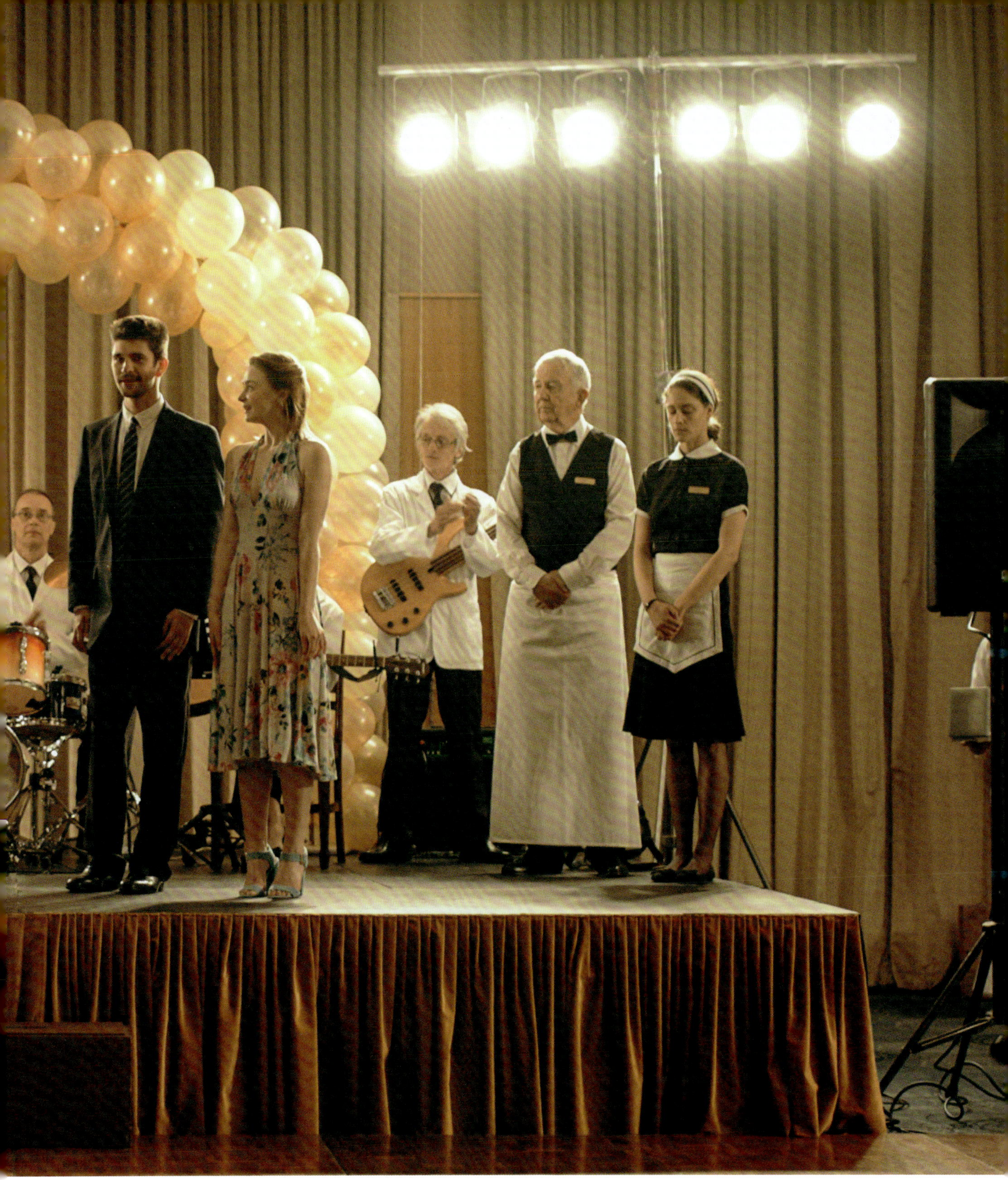

112

00:45:47

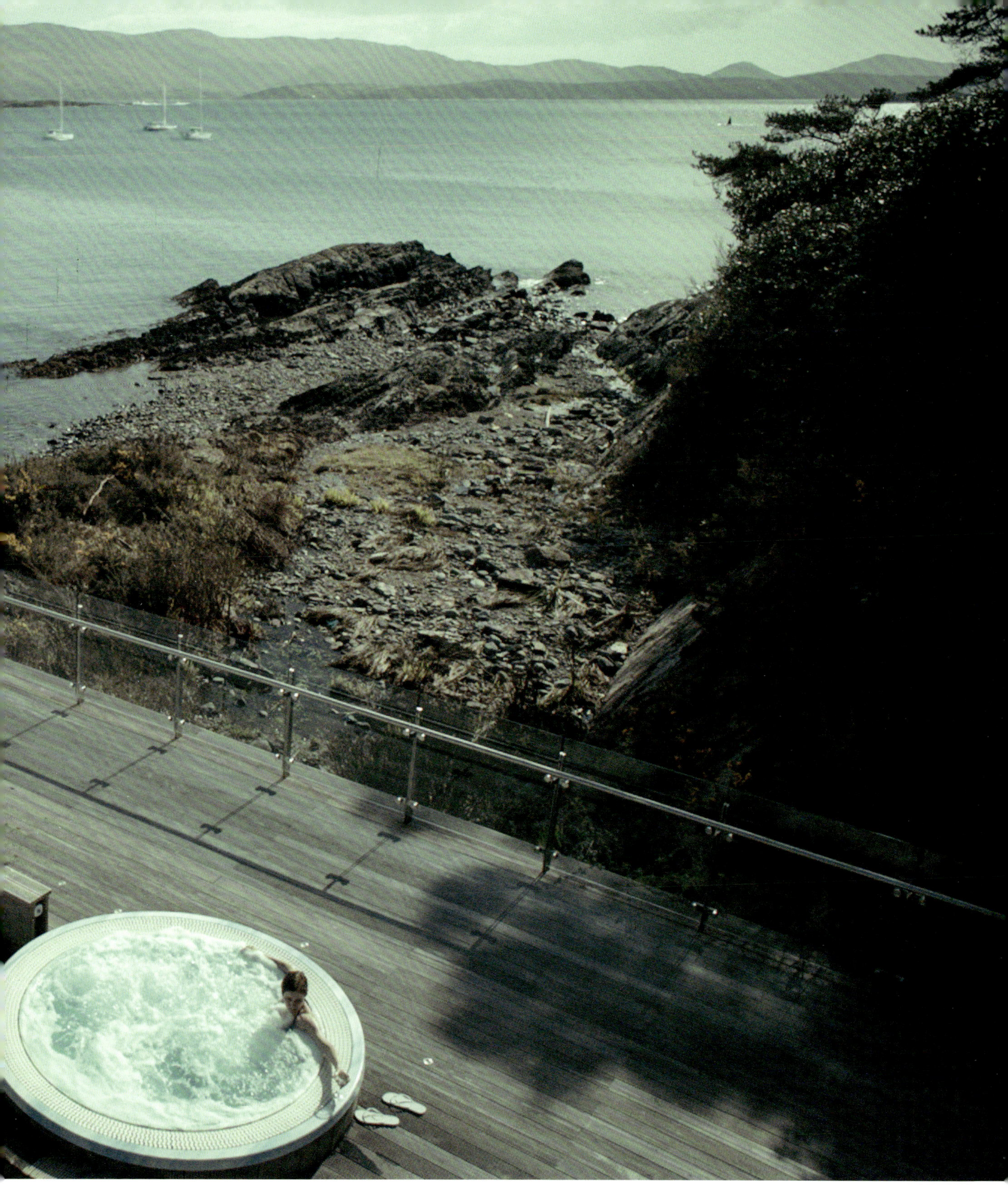

114

00:55:07

115

116

00:59:58

117

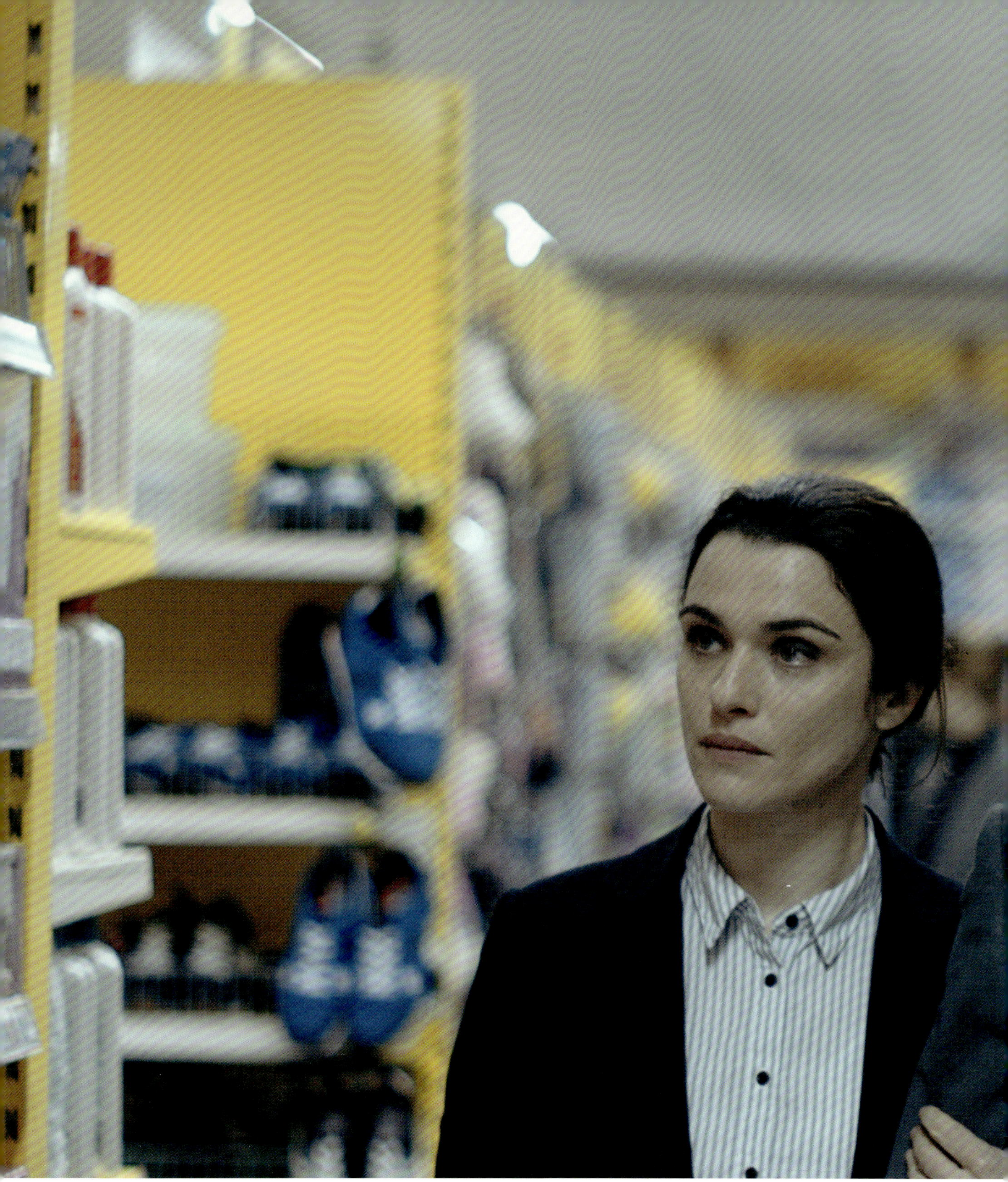

119

01:10:20

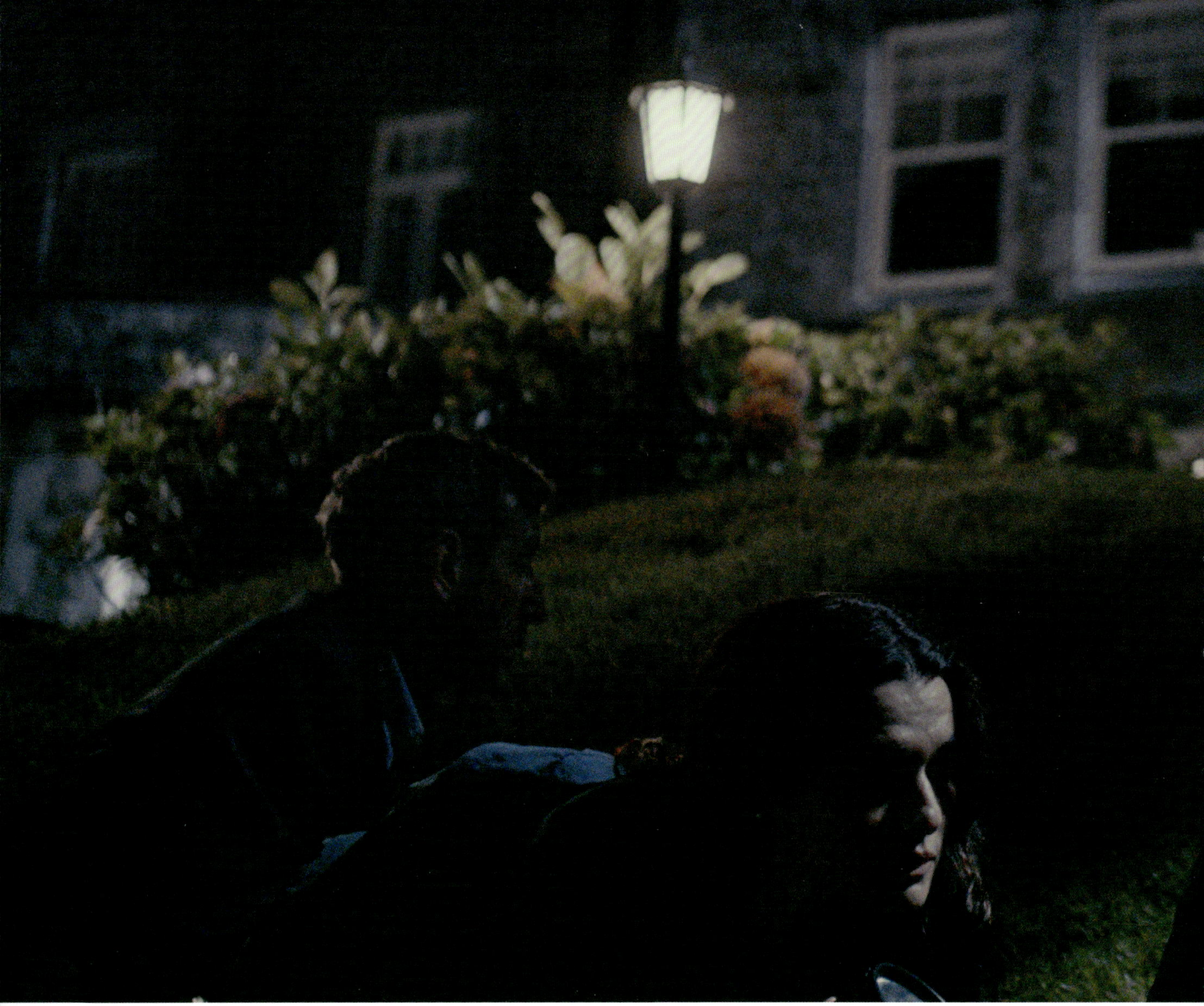

121

01:17:36

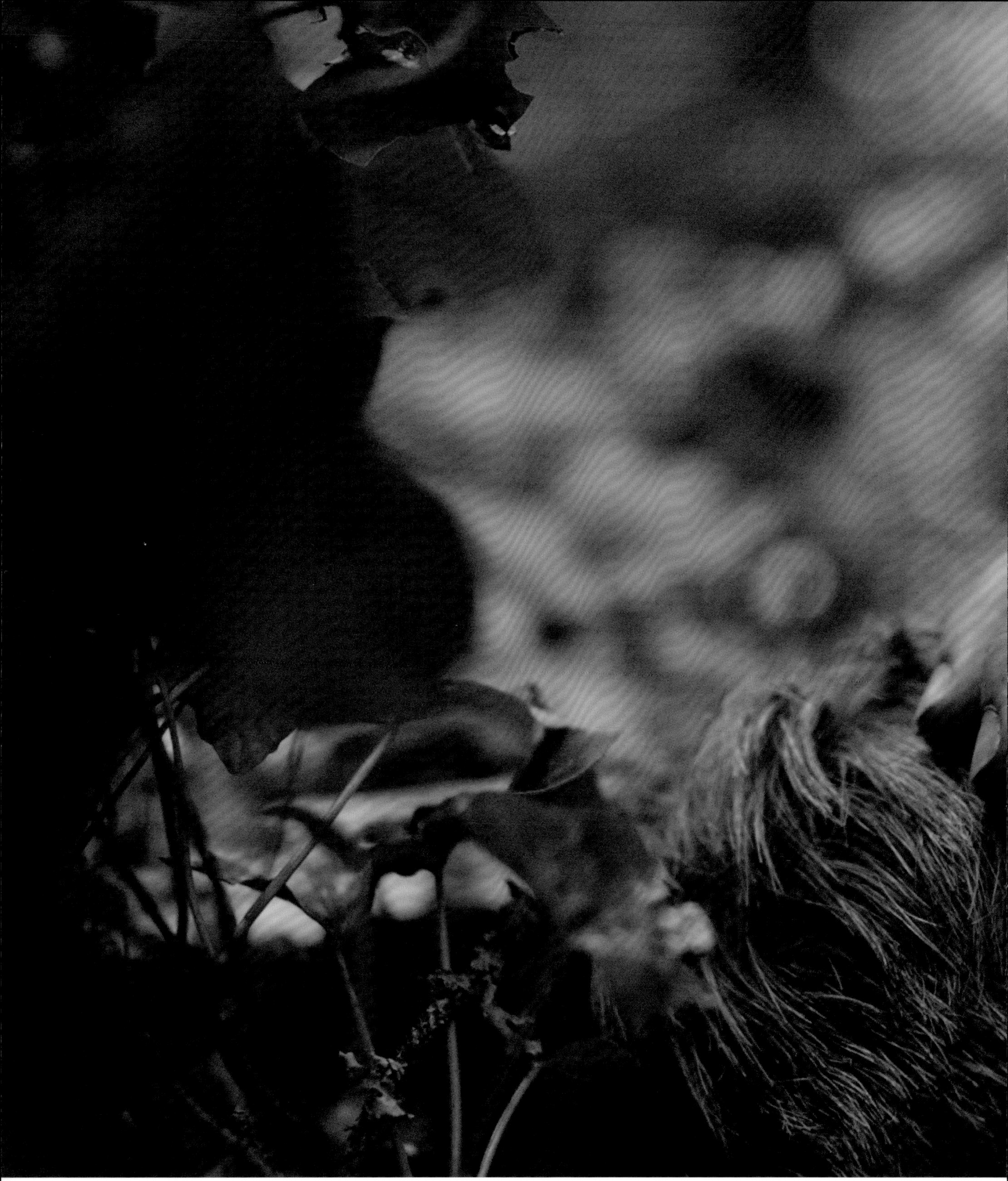

123

01:25:56

124

125

01:26:54

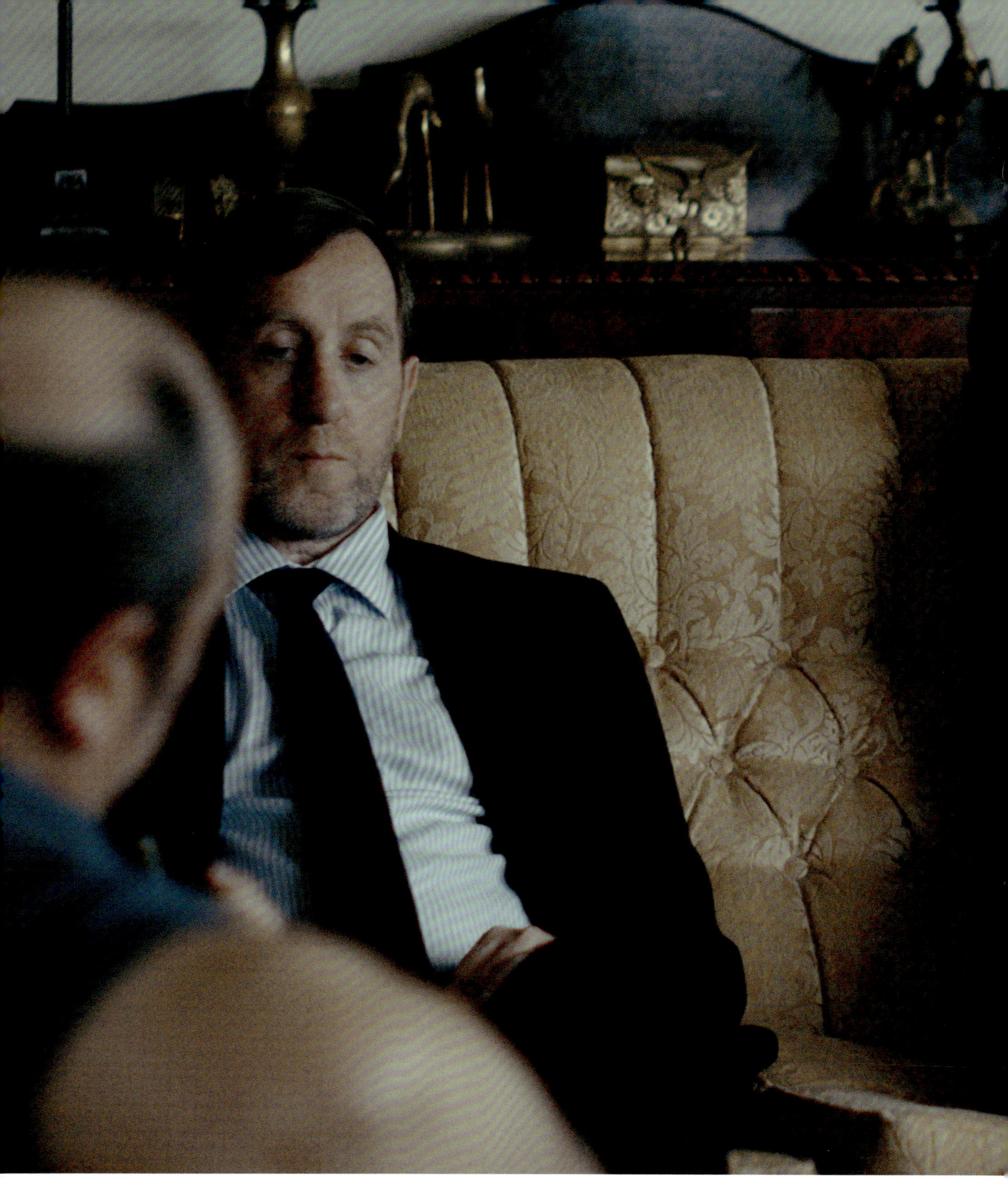

127

01:30:04

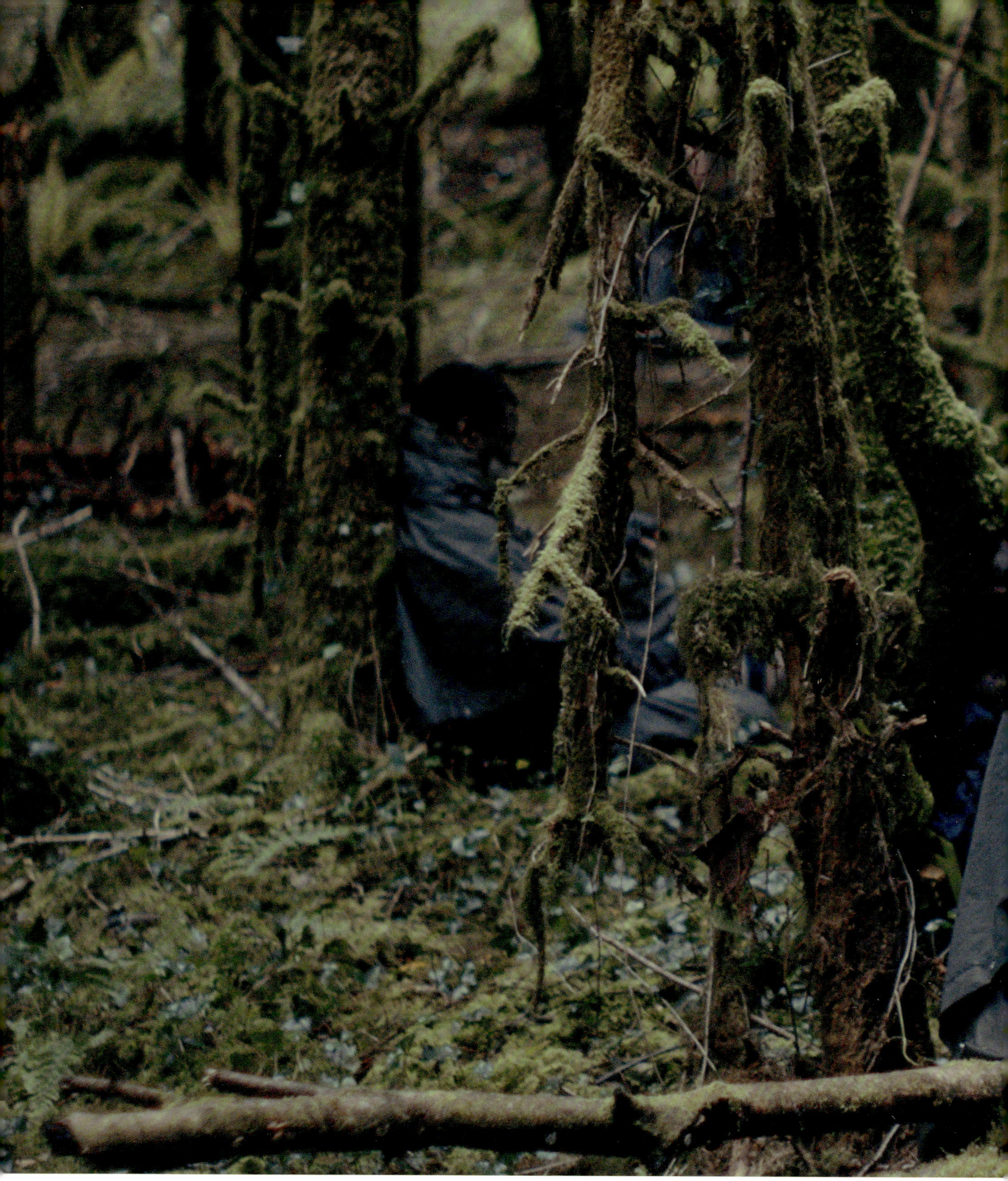

129

01:31:10

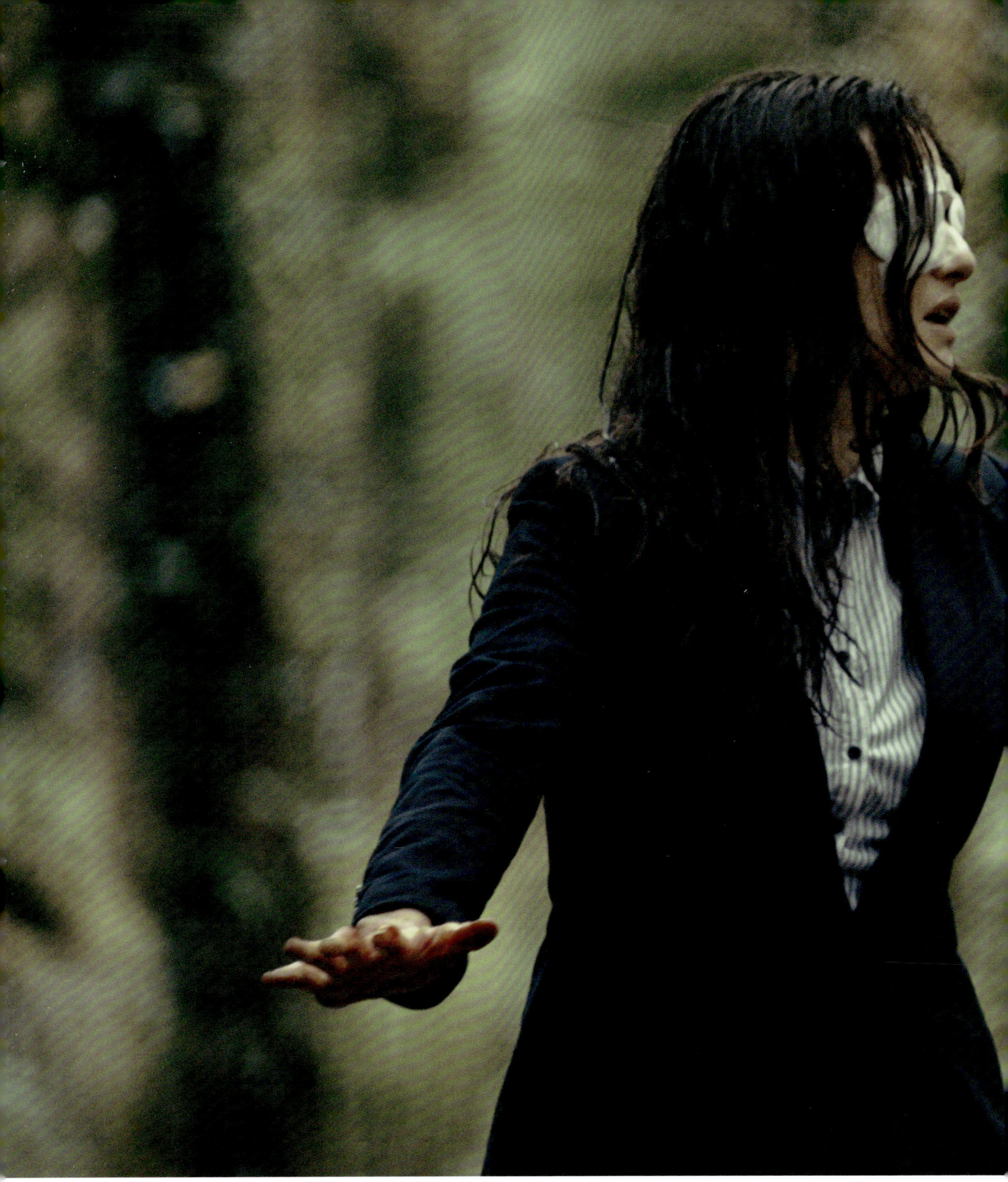

131

01:39:27

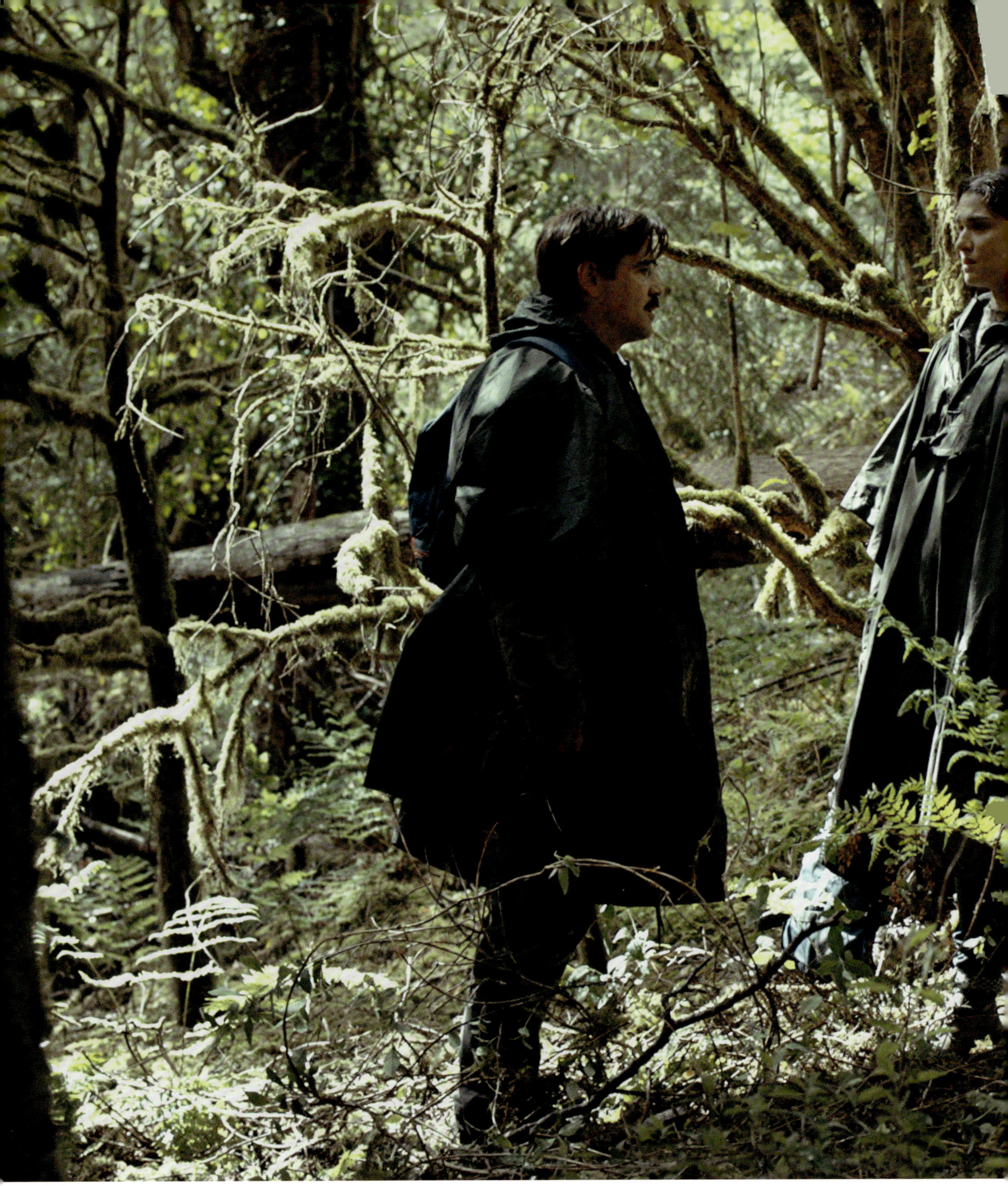

133

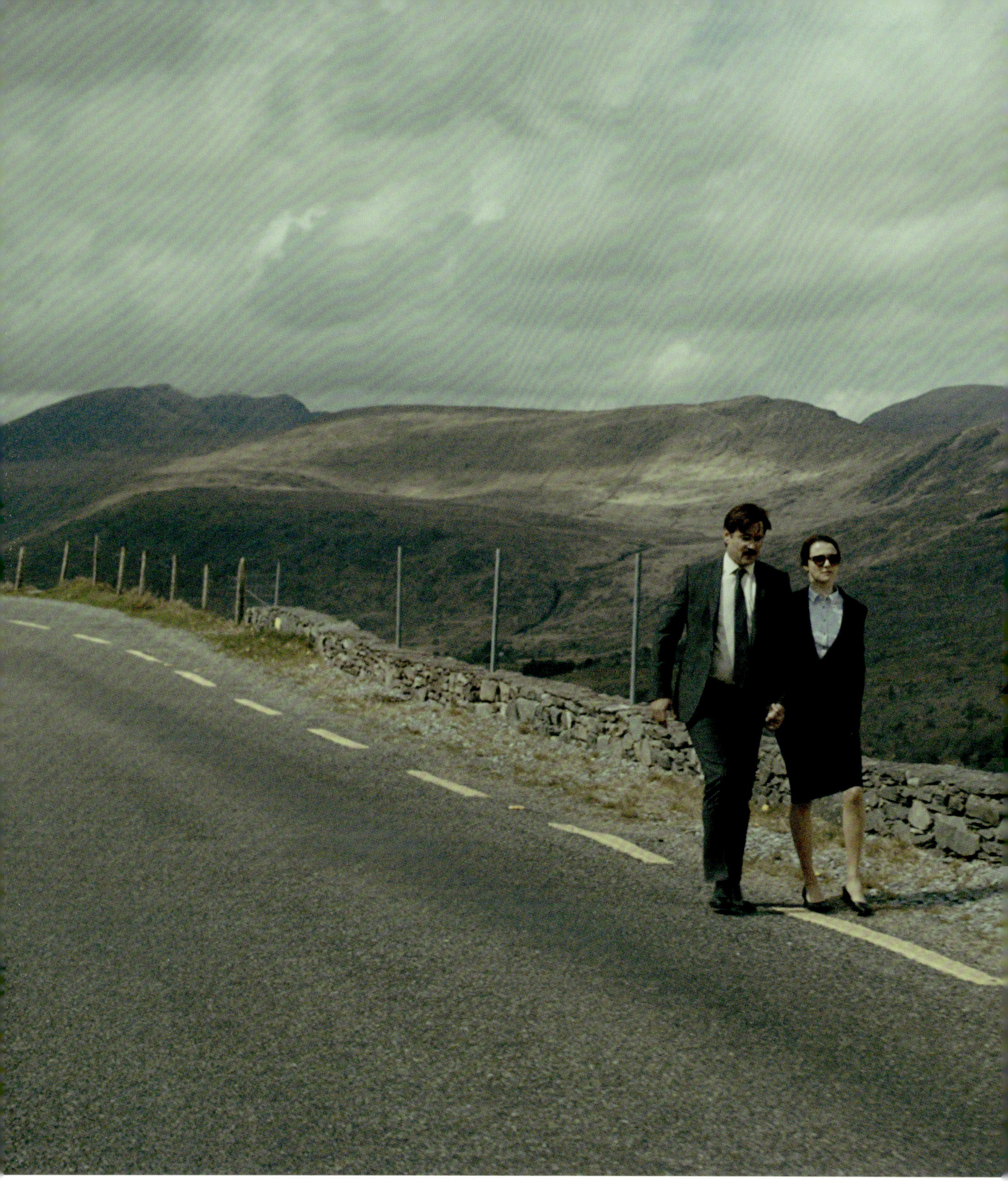

135

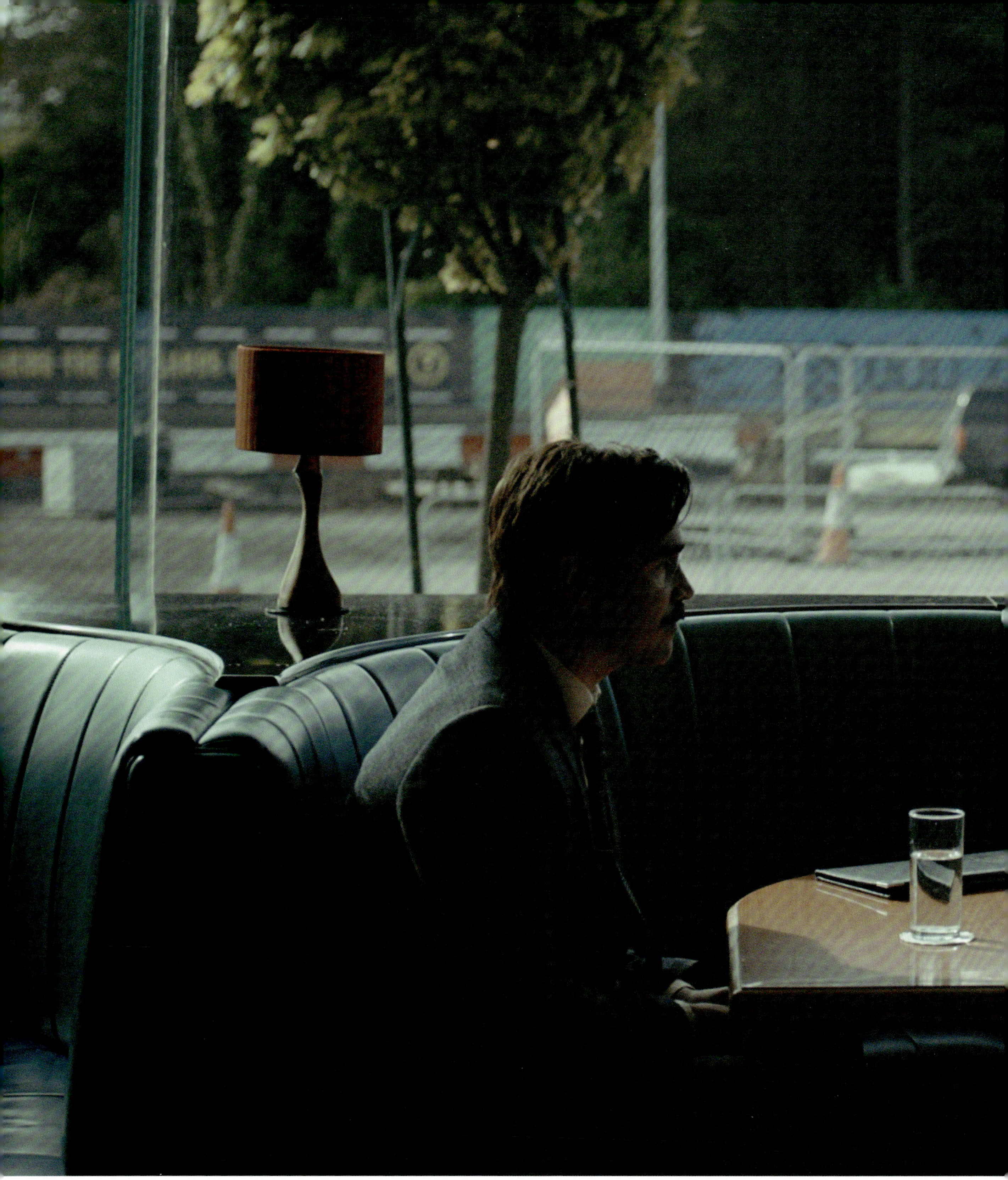

137

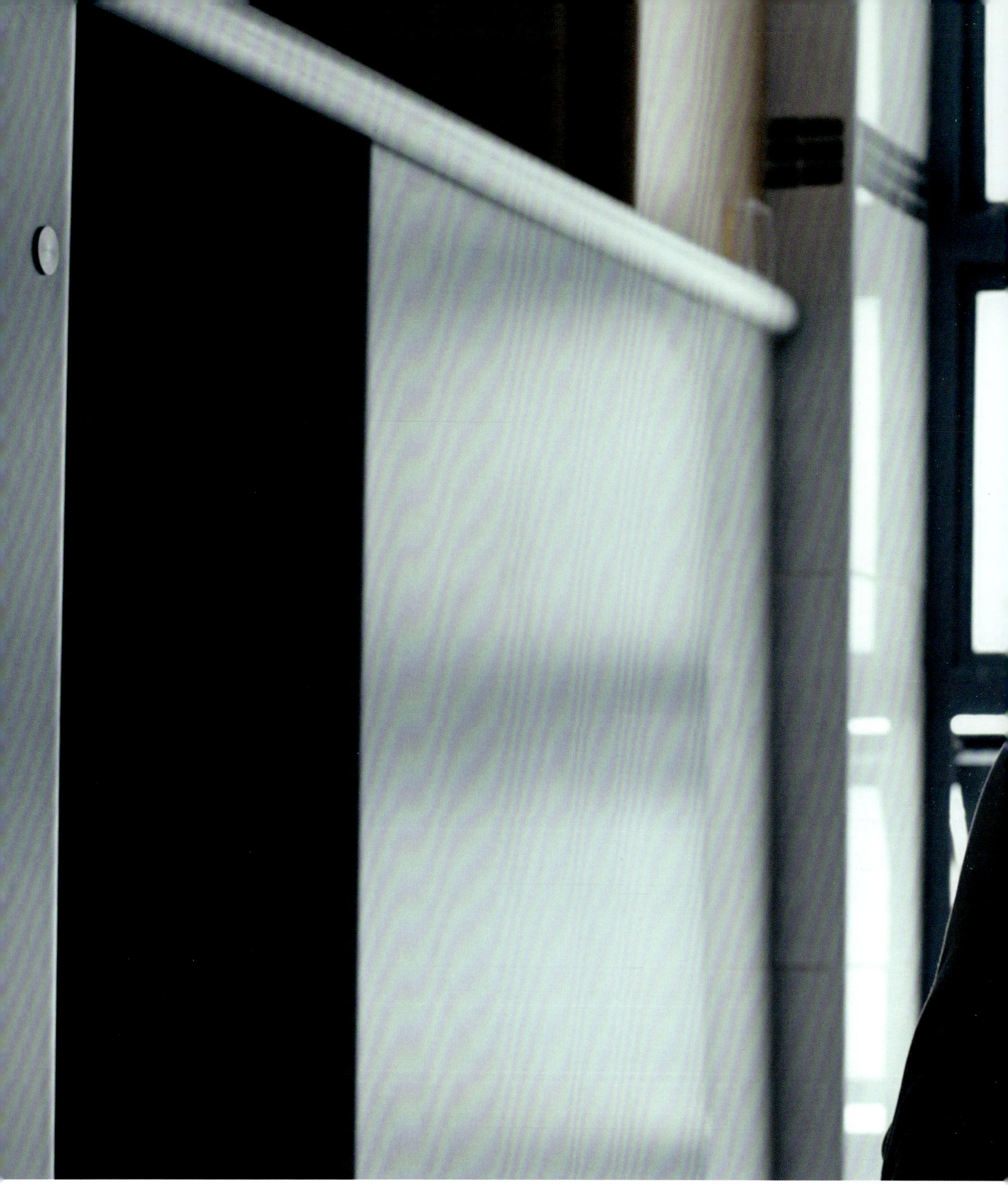

139

SECTION

III

BLINDED BY LOVE

Written by Ottessa Moshfegh

THE LOBSTER

"Lobsters live for one hundred years, are blue-blooded like aristocrats, and stay fertile all their lives. I also like the sea very much. I waterski and swim quite well, since I was a teenager," says David to the Hotel Manager. He has just arrived at the seaside hotel, where he has 45 days to find a suitable partner among the other hotel guests. If he fails, he will get turned into an animal—in this case a lobster—the creature he has chosen for himself. His brother, who accompanies him, has already been turned into a dog.

"Just think, as an animal you'll have a second chance to find a companion," the Hotel Manager tells him. "But even then you must be careful. You need to choose a companion that is a similar type of animal to you. A wolf and a penguin could never live together. Nor could a camel and a hippopotamus. That would be absurd. Think about it." In this warning lies the rub: It is illegal to be single here, and the only appropriately matched partners are individuals who share a specific attribute, a "defining characteristic." It's a surrealist take on some very true-to-life edicts. It took the United States until 1967 to decree that anti-miscegenation laws were illegal. Same-sex marriage is still illegal in many states today. But homosexuality isn't an issue at the Hotel, as long as you successfully partner up. Bisexuality wouldn't work, of course; you have to choose to pair with one gender or the other—limiting your options is the name of the game.

Not surprisingly, the uniforms that hotel guests wear are stereotypically gendered costumes of identical suits and dresses meant to obscure everything about a person except their defining characteristic, like having crooked teeth or, in the case of David, shortsightedness (he wears glasses). For the purpose of finding a mate, individuation is reduced to a single quirk, and each quirk has little to do with the pragmatics of chemistry in pairing people. The logic is, "Whatever you have in common is all that is special about you." It is the same principle in fascism, as it is exactly the celebration of commonality that creates the concept of "the other."

Maybe David's less-than-perfect vision has something to do with his choice of the lobster, too: A lobster's eyes are capable of distinguishing movement in dim light, but that's about all. Put a lobster in sunlight and he is completely blind (they mostly use their antennae as sensors). A lobster is an animal that we associate with being boiled alive. Lobster sex is devoid of intimacy: The male lobster puts a pair of pleopods into the female's stomach and releases his sperm. The female then releases her eggs to meet with the sperm at her discretion. Not very sexy. But maybe David's choice of the lobster is a way to protect himself from vulnerability. We learn at the beginning of the film that his wife has left him for another shortsighted man. This is why David is sent to the Hotel: he has been abandoned. A lobster has a hard exoskeleton to protect itself from predators and claws that can exert pressure of up to 100 pounds per square inch, enough to easily break a human finger. Furthermore, the lobster lacks the brain anatomy needed to feel pain. So one might gather that David is, in addition to being shortsighted, not all that interested in sensuality, or joy, or richness of experience, or personal growth. David is interested in solitude and murk.

We begin the film expecting David to fail to find love because we're not sure David is capable of real love. His flat affect seems evidence of this. All characters in *The Lobster* speak formally, as though they are translating their real thoughts and feelings into a mode of speech that deflects their actual truth. There is no tonal distinction between The Receptionist and Nosebleed Woman, for example. The former says to David upon his arrival at the Hotel, "You're not allowed to use the basketball or volleyball courts, these are only for the couples. You can use the facilities for individual sports, such as squash and golf," and the latter says while dancing with David, "I'm sorry, I've got blood on you. But don't worry. There are many ways to remove blood stains from clothes quite easily. One is to wash the item in cold water and then rub it with sea salt. Another is to scrub the stains with cotton wool dipped in ammonia." Later, when Nosebleed Woman is eating dinner on a yacht with her new companion Limping Man and Elizabeth, their "child," the conversation is just as stiff:

```
                LIMPING MAN
A basketball weighs between 550 and 650
grams. Did you know that?

               NOSEBLEED WOMAN
No, I didn't know that.

                LIMPING MAN
Yes. Its weight is different for men's
and women's games, but that's rough-
ly how much they weigh. Do you know how
much a volleyball weighs?

                 ELIZABETH
No, but I'd love to find out.
```

Their repartee is trivial in the most literal definition of the word. And I think that's the hard-wrung, dark humor of the film's comedic moments; if it wasn't so tedious and depressing, I'd laugh.

But the flatness has a deeper meaning within the universe of the film. To be completely measured and deadpan is a very difficult thing to do; one mustn't telegraph any of their interior life on their face; one's voice must never be too expressive. One must *act*, essentially, instead of simply *be*. The affect is a learned mechanism of the fascistic society in which these characters attempt to exist. It is not safe to be honest, or candid, or truly vulnerable; one must behave according to the norm or lose one's humanity, literally. If one person were to defy the standard, rebel against the system, others might, too—so communication and self-characterization are controlled and censored. We get the sense that the hotel walls have ears and eyes. When Lisping Man masturbates in his room, the administration knows about it and publicly punishes him by putting his hand in a toaster during breakfast. The supreme mandate here is that everyone needs someone. So if you do for yourself what someone else can do unto you, you are going against the State.

Because there are no shortsighted women at the Hotel, David takes on a new defining characteristic, "heartlessness," and almost succeeds in scamming the system by pretending to be a sociopath in order to partner with a truly heartless woman (called Heartless Woman). Of course, his metaphorical shortsightedness fails him here. He can't actually be something he is not. David's emotional break, the major turning point in the film, occurs after Heartless Woman murders his dog-brother. It's a test, not of devotion, but of honesty. If David expresses anything, he will reveal himself as not a completely heartless man, thereby ruining his chances of marrying Heartless Woman. (The lobster is coming for him.) In this scene we understand his enactment of flatness in the face of grief and horror as a form of survival. It's a meaningful moment in the script; we see the protagonist fold, however slightly, under the pressure of the game. David cries at the sight of the bloody dog, a mistake which eventually leads to him escaping from the Hotel and joining the "Loners" in the woods.

There's something noble, of course, in choosing to be single and free; Americans like me pride ourselves on our "independence." I think most of us would want to run away and join the Loners in the woods rather than leash ourselves to someone whose partnership demands a reduction of self to one principal characteristic. I know I would. Our sympathy for the Loners is thus easily earned. They are the underdogs, freedom fighters in rugged camping gear, until their Leader proves to be just as cruel, if not more so, than her counterpart in the land of luxury and partnership, the Hotel Manager. And in truth, the Loners are not free; the people at the Hotel hunt them with tranquilizer guns, each captured body earning them an extra day at the Hotel. Furthermore, the Loners have their own fascistic rules: no romantic relationships, no flirting. Kissing is punished by the slashing of one's lips; coitus by the slashing of one's genitals. If your leg gets caught in a bear trap, that's your problem. You dig your own grave. It's every man and woman for him or herself. Yes, even the rebels are extreme in their purity and self-regulation (as rebels often are). The film seems to suggest that societies are born out of self-regulation, and that humanity itself—what separates us from the animals, say—is defined by our ability to control ourselves and our baser instincts. We are not slaves to lust or fantasy. We are intelligent. We are deliberate and reasonable. We can choose to love who we want and to be what we want.

Despite the hardcore savageness of the Loners, I am weirdly drawn to their kind of discipline. I was never all that interested in partnership until I met the man I ended up marrying. I grew up believing that marriage was a necessarily sexist institution, and to submit to it was to surrender

SECTION III

one's will and intelligence to someone who didn't deserve it, because no one should have power over anyone. I believed that love was a force beyond our control, like beauty or death. Marriage was the corruption of romantic love, I thought. Why get married? What's the big fuss? Evidence tells us that marriage has been around for about four thousand years. Before the institution began, anthropologists say, we lived in a more tribal manner. Hunter-gatherers lived in groups led by several men. The men shared the women and had children who went on to do the same. It's so completely unromantic—and yet romance is such an enormous part of the human experience. We crave it and search for it. Romantic love is the panacea for a world that seems otherwise material and hard. When David finds Shortsighted Woman among the Loners, we want them to fall in love, even though it puts them in a very dangerous situation. In fact, that's what makes it so exciting.

There is a town in *The Lobster*, and it is just as terrifying to me as the Hotel. The city scenes were shot in Dublin, a town I like a lot. But the way the landscape is captured mimics a kind of futuristic, post-apocalyptic civilization, one strangely out of human scale. When David, Shortsighted Woman, Loner Leader, and Loner Swimmer go to the Town to buy necessities—they also share cake— we see them dressed as professionals, tidy and prim. They look like good citizens, walking arm in arm, content but not happy. Determined, but not overly zealous. Curious, but not hungry. They go to a shopping mall where we witness police trolling for suspected Loners. While David is left alone, an officer demands to see his marriage certificate. Shortsighted Woman comes to the rescue, kissing him on the lips: "I'm sorry, darling." They are clearly a couple, so the cop lets them go. So far, they have only been pretending to be in love. At this moment, in the face of tyranny, however, the farce earns real value. Perhaps it is the rebellion against the Loner credo that makes their love affair so exciting. Or perhaps they fall in love despite the ruse, honestly, as though they were meant for one another. It's impossible to know for sure. But they are free as long as they are tied to each other.

Soon they decide to break from the Loners and join society as man and wife. In a tragic twist, Loner Leader brings Shortsighted Woman to an eye doctor. She is blinded, in order to sabotage her shared characteristic with her sweetheart, David. By the end of the film, the lovers confront a horrifying truth: The only way to stay together is for David to blind himself as well. They escape to the Town alone and sit at a roadside diner, where David asks their waiter for a steak knife and goes to the toilets.

```
INT. TOWN RESTAURANT TOILETS - DAY

David pulls lots of paper towels out
of the dispenser. He tucks them
into his shirt collar and lays them
over his shoulders to keep the blood
off. He looks at himself in the
mirror, checks to see if his hands
are trembling and then raises the
knife, bringing it close to his
eye. Closer and closer. He can't do
it, and lowers the knife again.
He then takes a few deep breaths and
tries again.
```

The film ends with a long shot of Shortsighted Woman alone at the table, waiting, as we are, for David's return. The first time I watched this film, I thought, yes, maybe love is powerful enough to make a man gouge out his own eyes. Wouldn't that be proof? He should do it. In fact, he's an asshole if he doesn't. Now I feel differently; I want him to put the knife down, to realize that his affection for this woman is a delusion. I want him to walk away. Would I gouge my eyes out for love? No. Because I know I shouldn't have to. Ironically, since I first saw the film, I fell in love and got married.

It was New Year's Eve, 2018. That morning, Luke and I called up a marriage service and ordered an officiant to come marry us that afternoon in our East Hollywood apartment. Then we went to the jewelry district in Downtown Los Angeles to buy rings. Afterward, we stopped for frozen yogurt. I remember we argued about something trivial, both a bit on edge. When we got home, we showered and dressed and picked up the apartment just in time for the woman sent by the service to read us the prescribed oath and pronounce us man and wife. We did have to provide identification and fill in a certificate that required the names and birthplaces of our parents. But that was all. Nobody asked about our personalities, our goals, our likes and dislikes. Nobody evaluated our appearances, our voices, the length of our hair. Only our own judgment and will would be to blame if the marriage failed. We paid extra to be married without a witness. It was five hundred dollars. Five hundred dollars and we were legally bound to one another. I didn't have to prove anything. I didn't have to gouge out my eyes. All I did was say "I do." Because I did.

In the world of *The Lobster*, what Luke and I have in common might be that we are high-functioning yet unbalanced people. "Crooked pots with crooked lids," as Luke's grandmother liked to say. Or maybe it would be that we both have big noses. We're both writers. Honestly, between two people there will always be a shared characteristic, like having long fingers or an allergy to fruit. It is simply a matter of how you define yourself, which trait you choose to spotlight in your life. Yes, we all might maim ourselves in order to share the same weakness as our partner. We all might lie and manipulate someone we want to love us. It is true that love blinds us, that love is dangerous and obscene, and that it will alienate you from whatever society you live in. And maybe it is also bullshit. The ambiguity of *The Lobster* allows for this possibility, which is why I can watch it over and over again, and each time I see it in a new way. I like to think of this film as a litmus test for how one understands partnership. Either *The Lobster* makes a lot of sense, or it makes no sense at all, and therein lies its profound wisdom and comedy.

Ottessa Moshfegh is the author of the novels *Death in Her Hands, My Year of Rest and Relaxation,* and *Eileen.*

SECTION

IV

SECTION IV

ON SET

Photos by Yorgos Lanthimos

THE LOBSTER

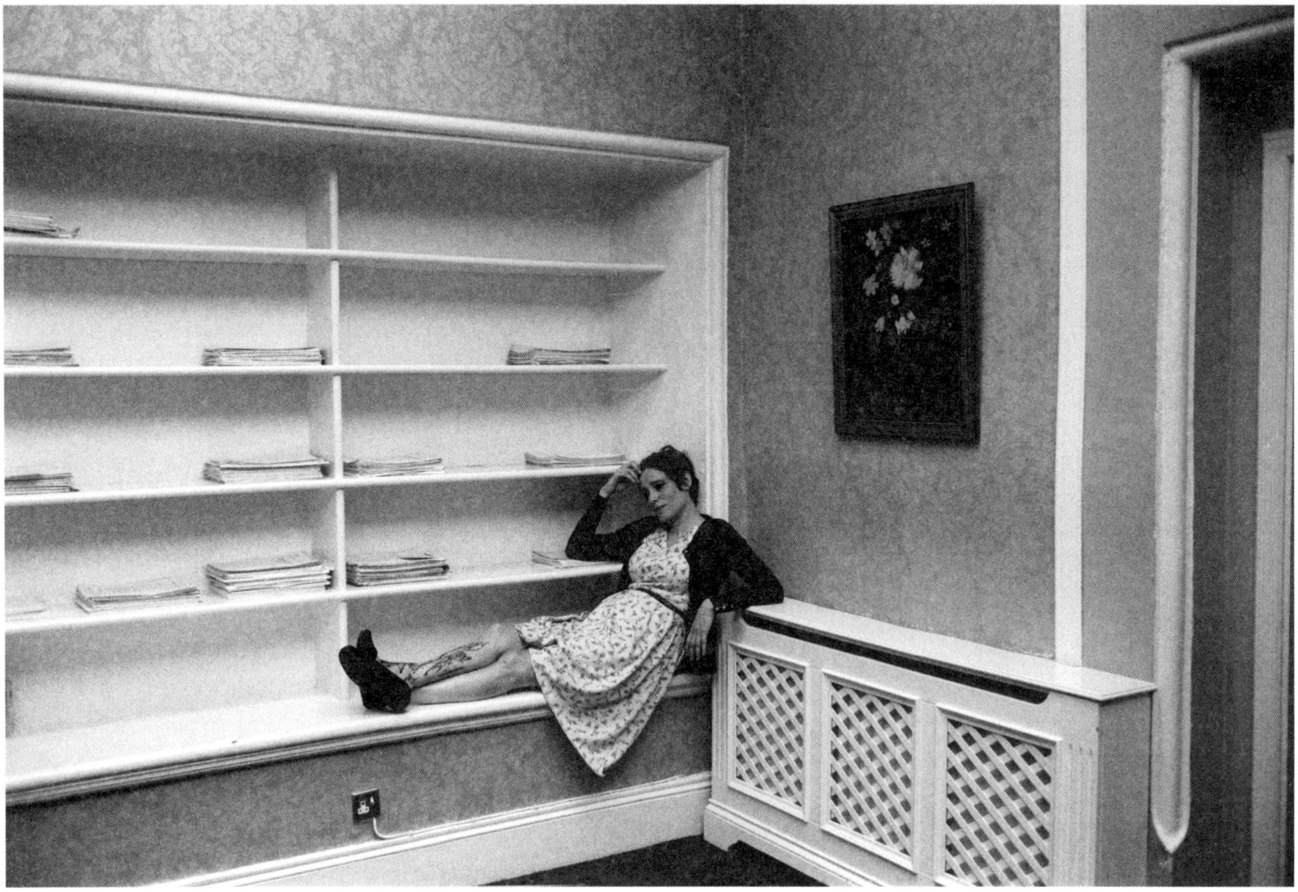

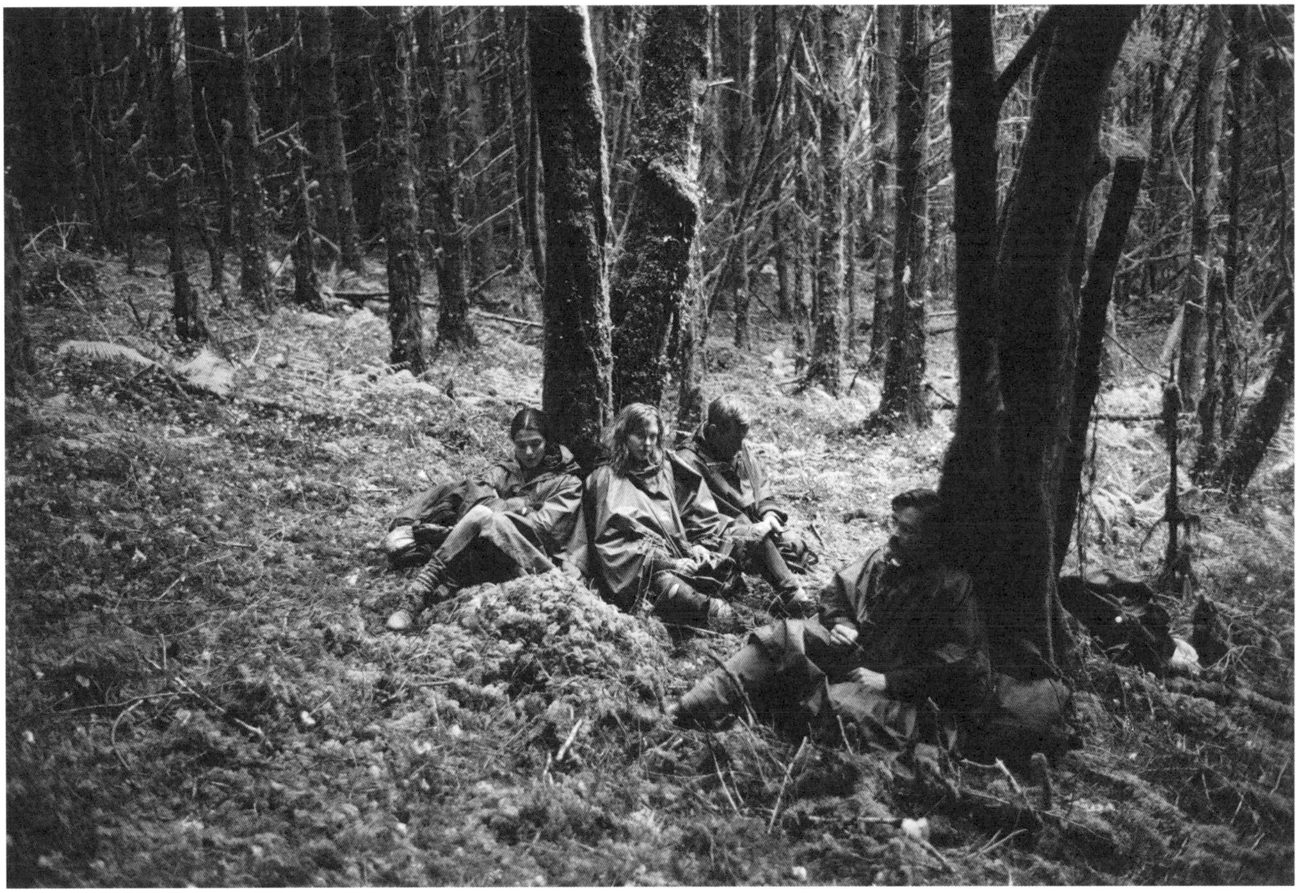

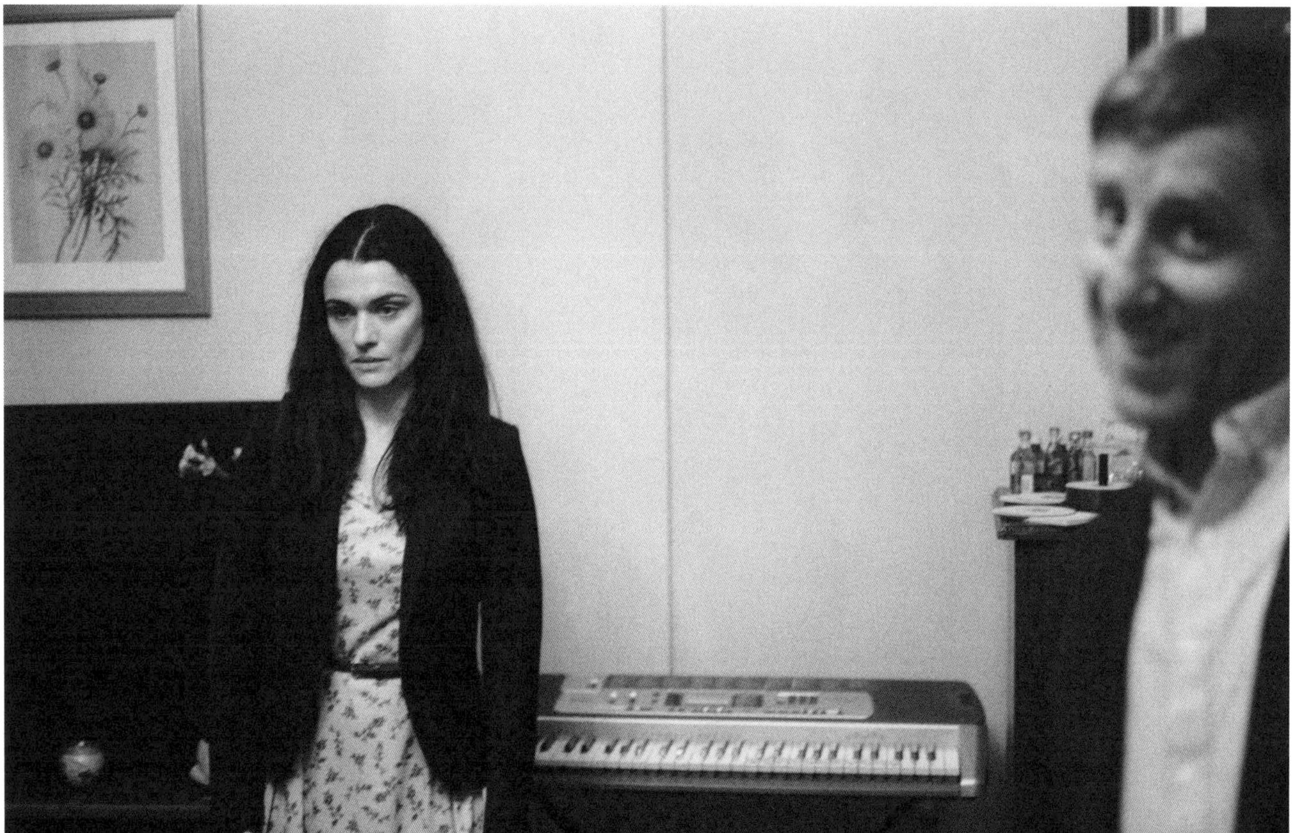

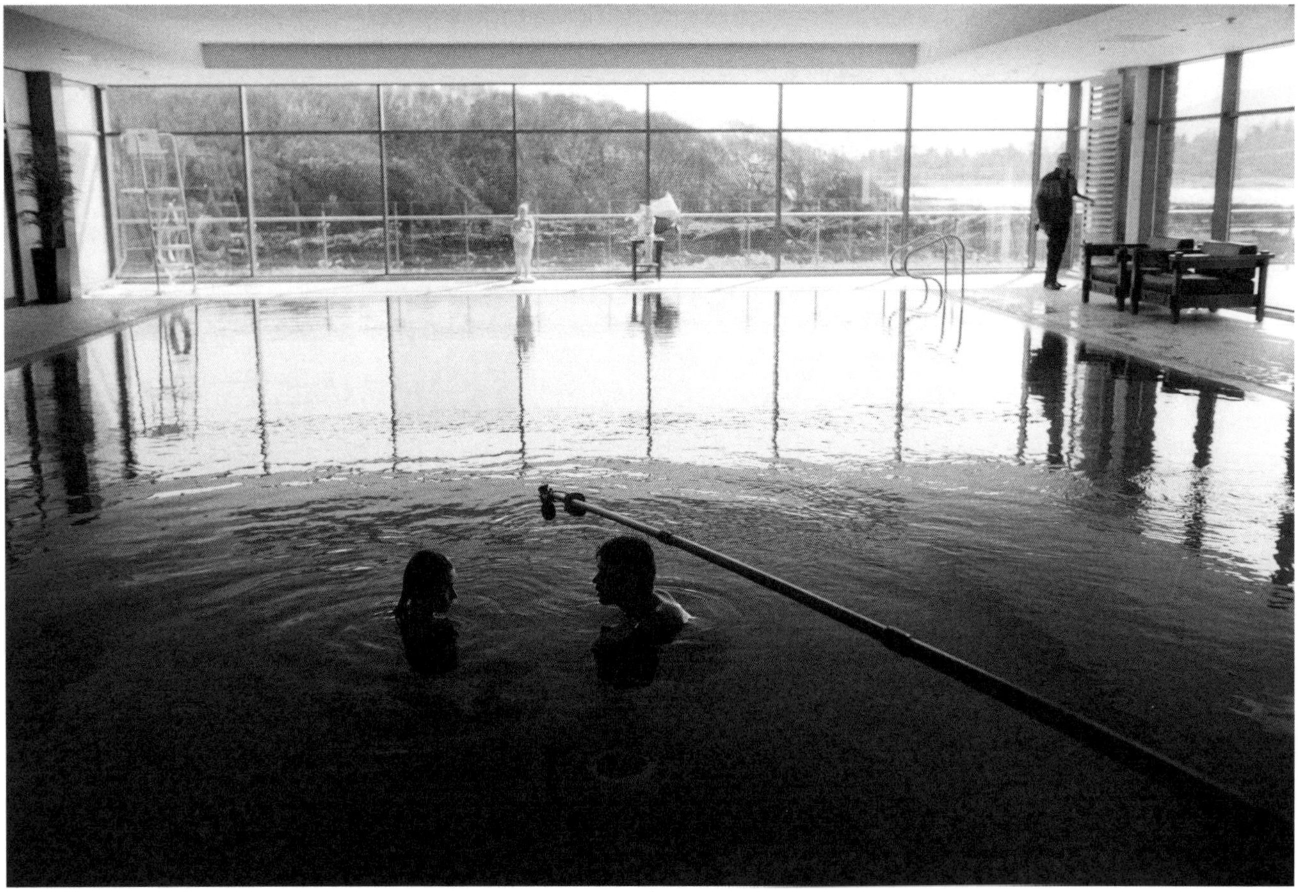

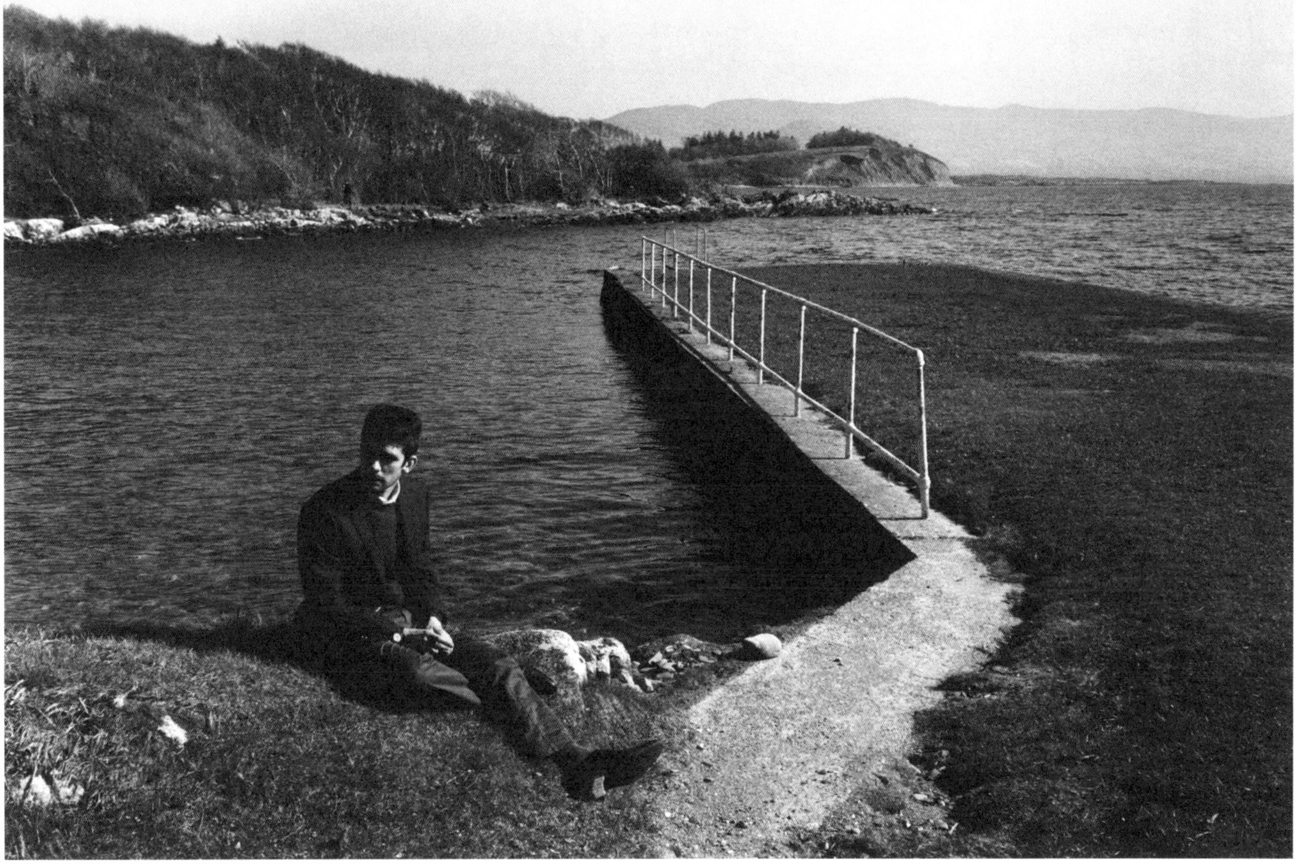

161

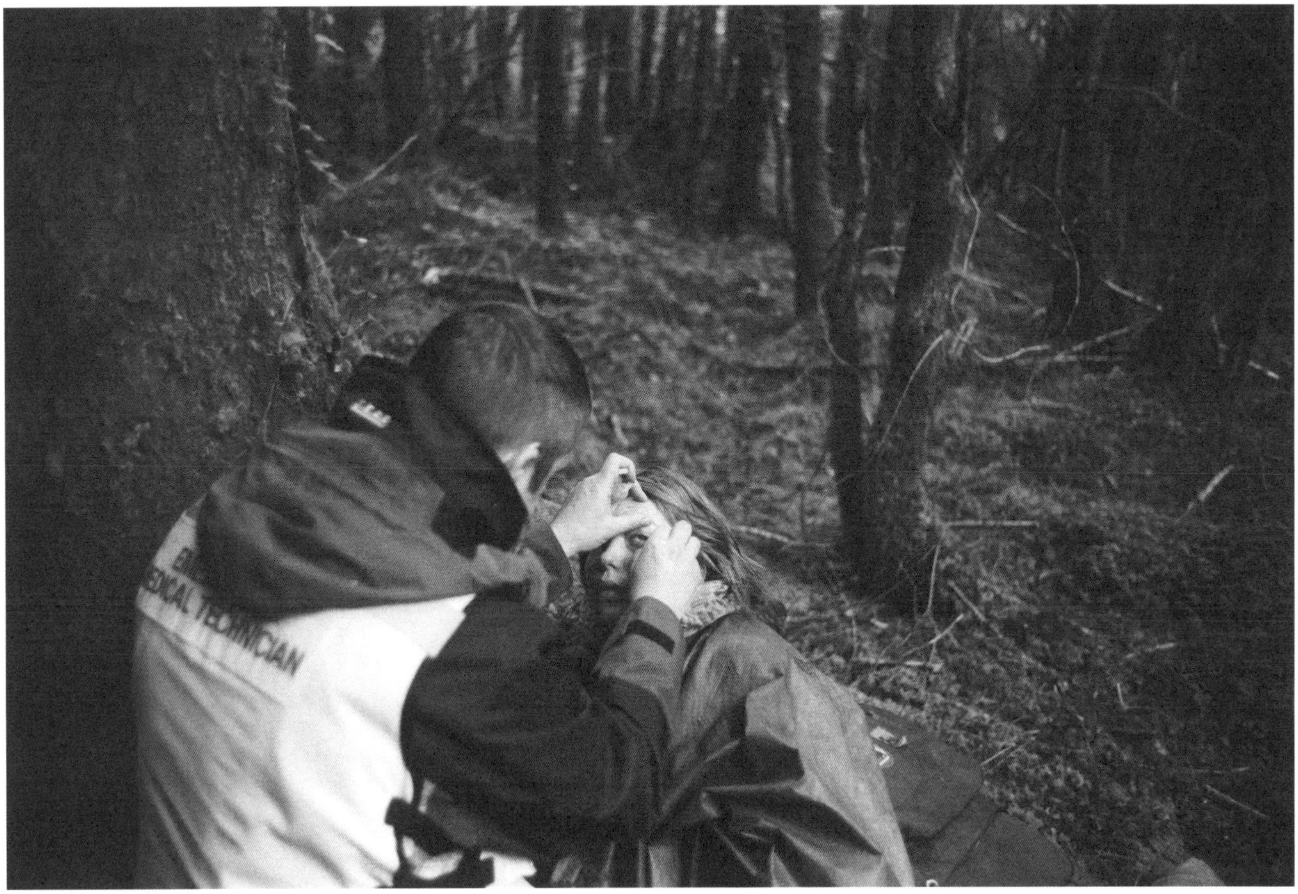
DICAL TECHNICIAN

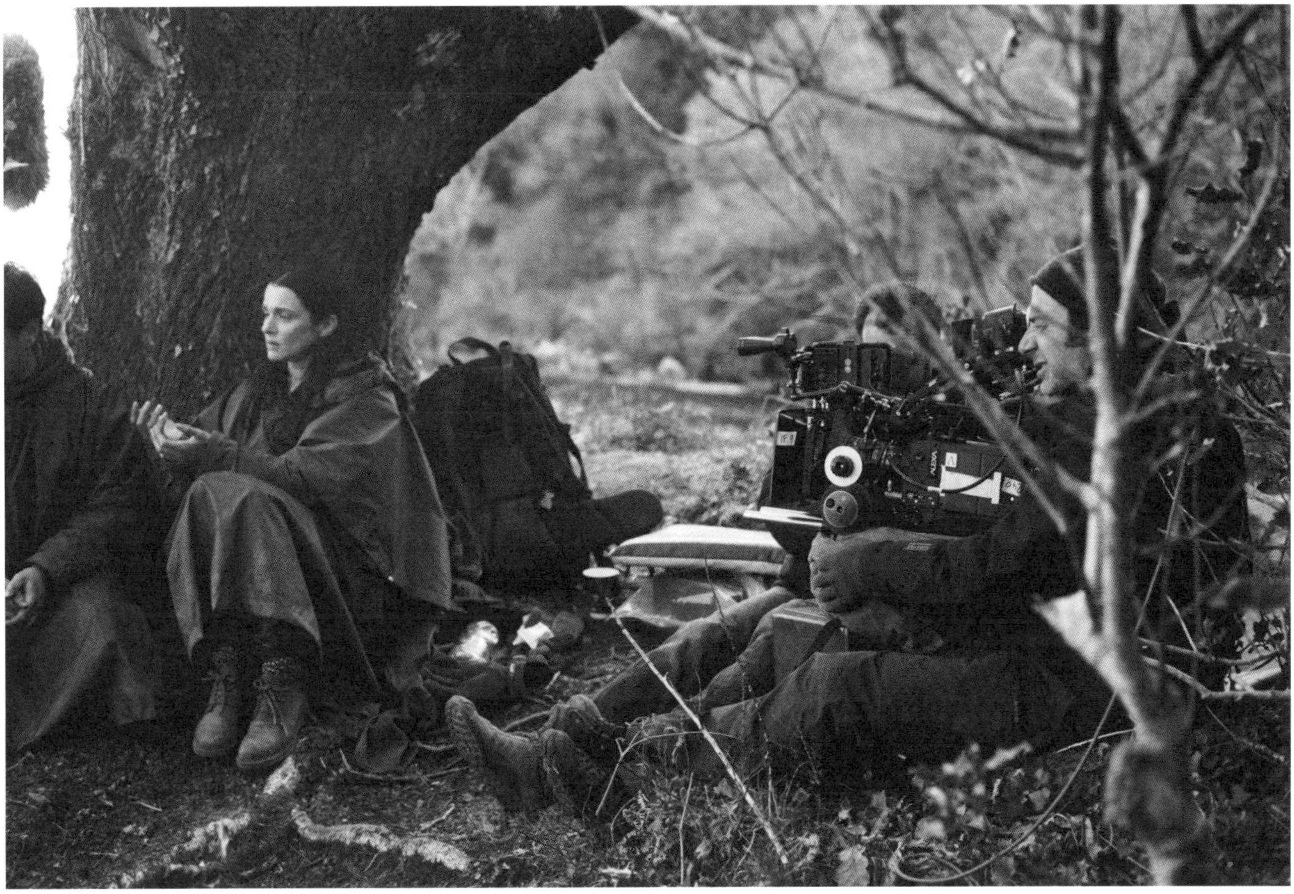

164

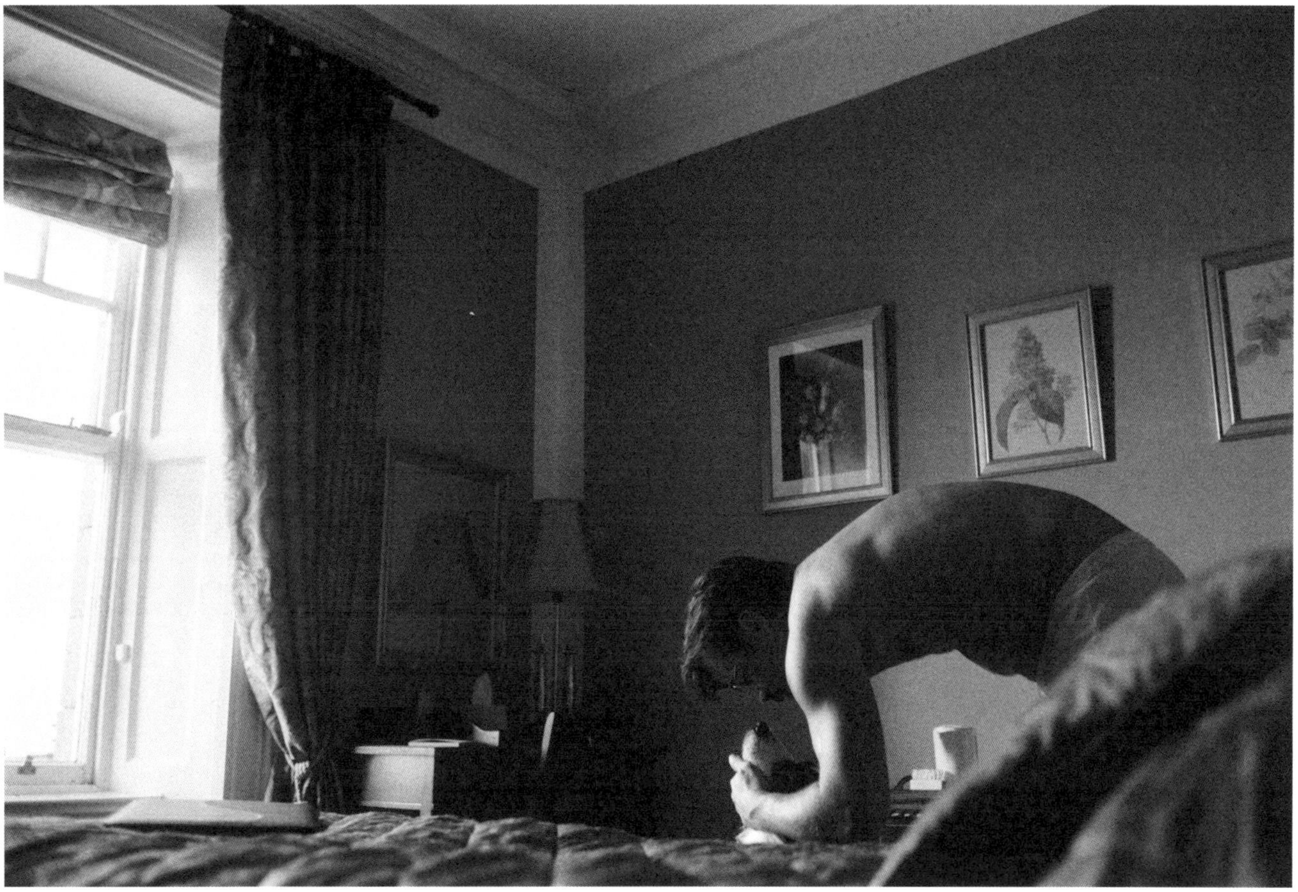

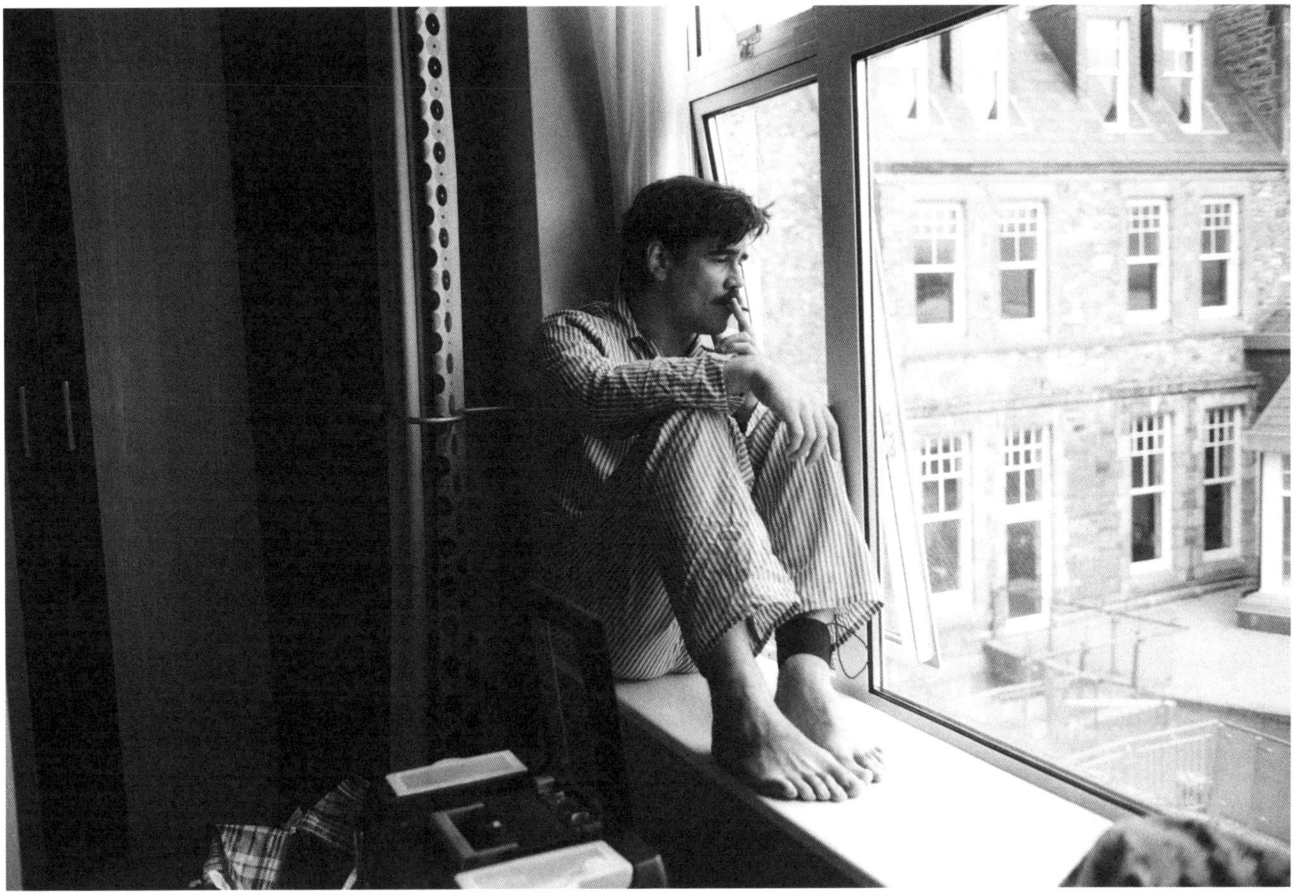

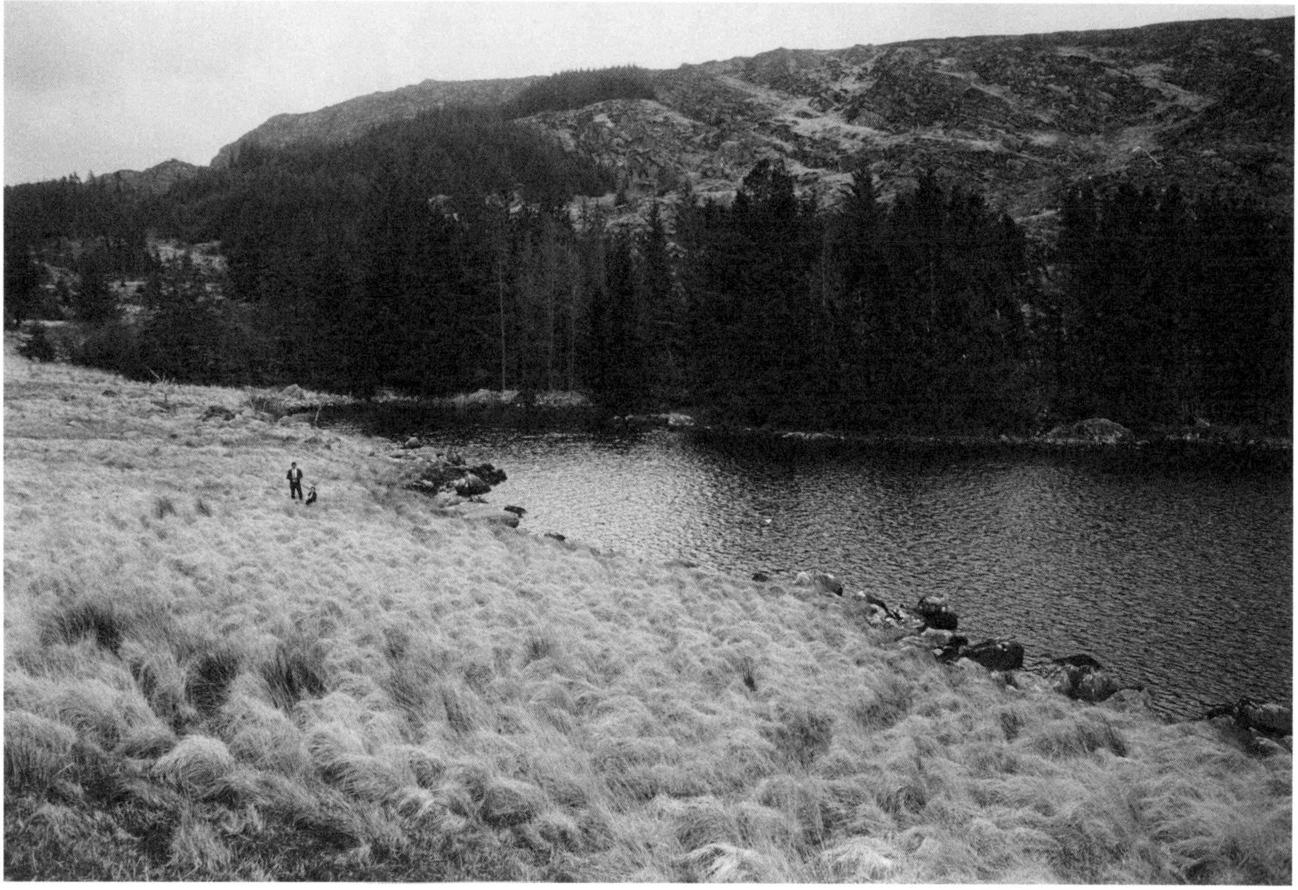

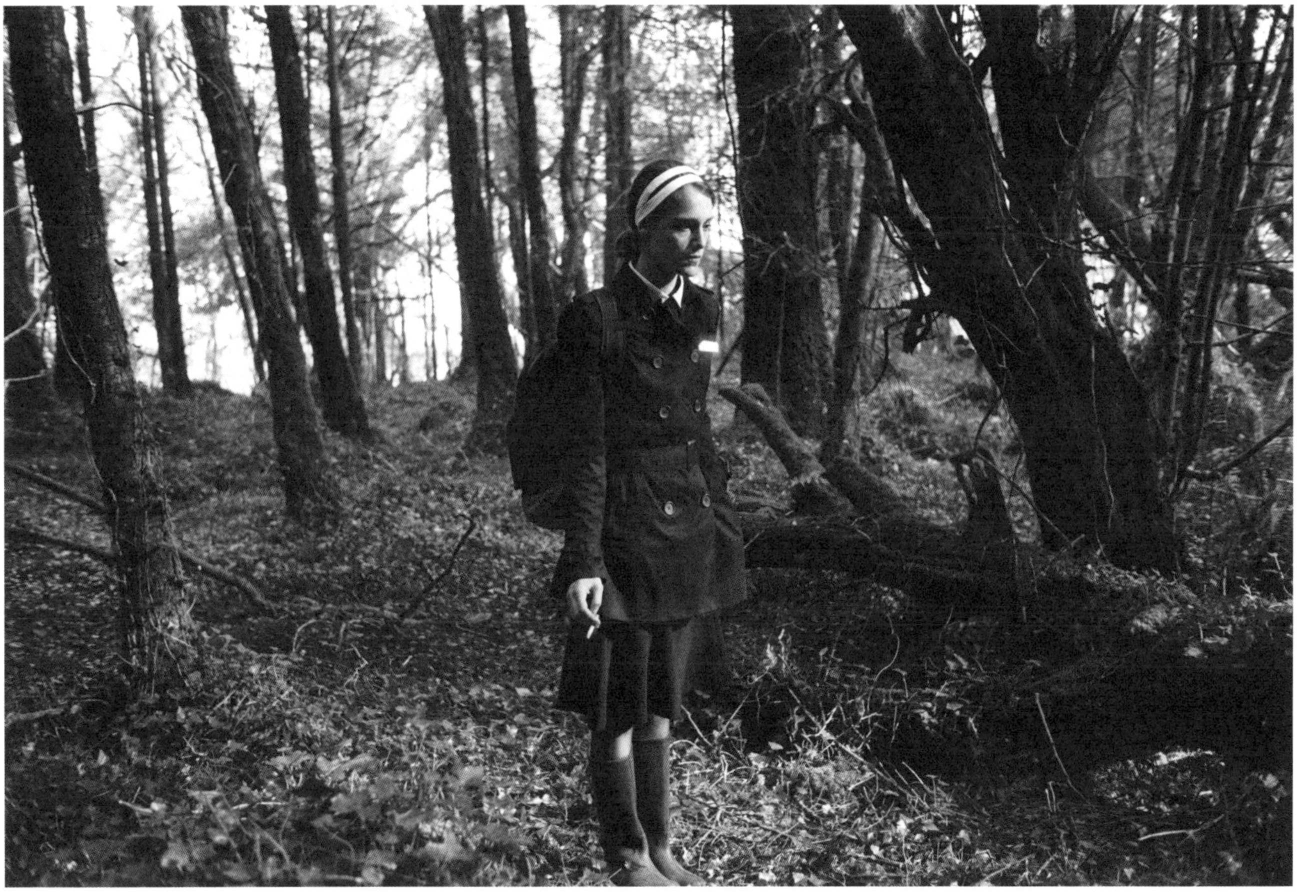

169

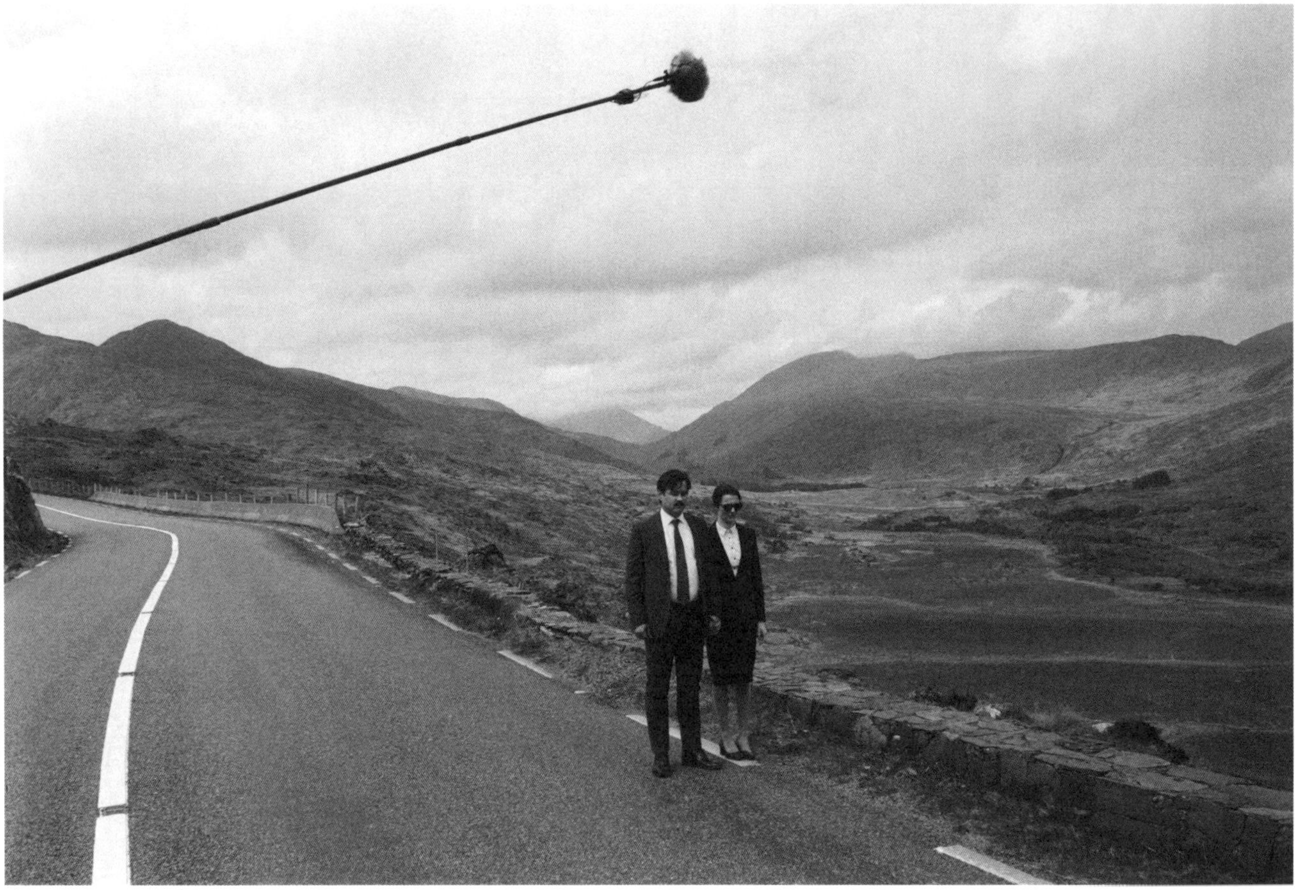

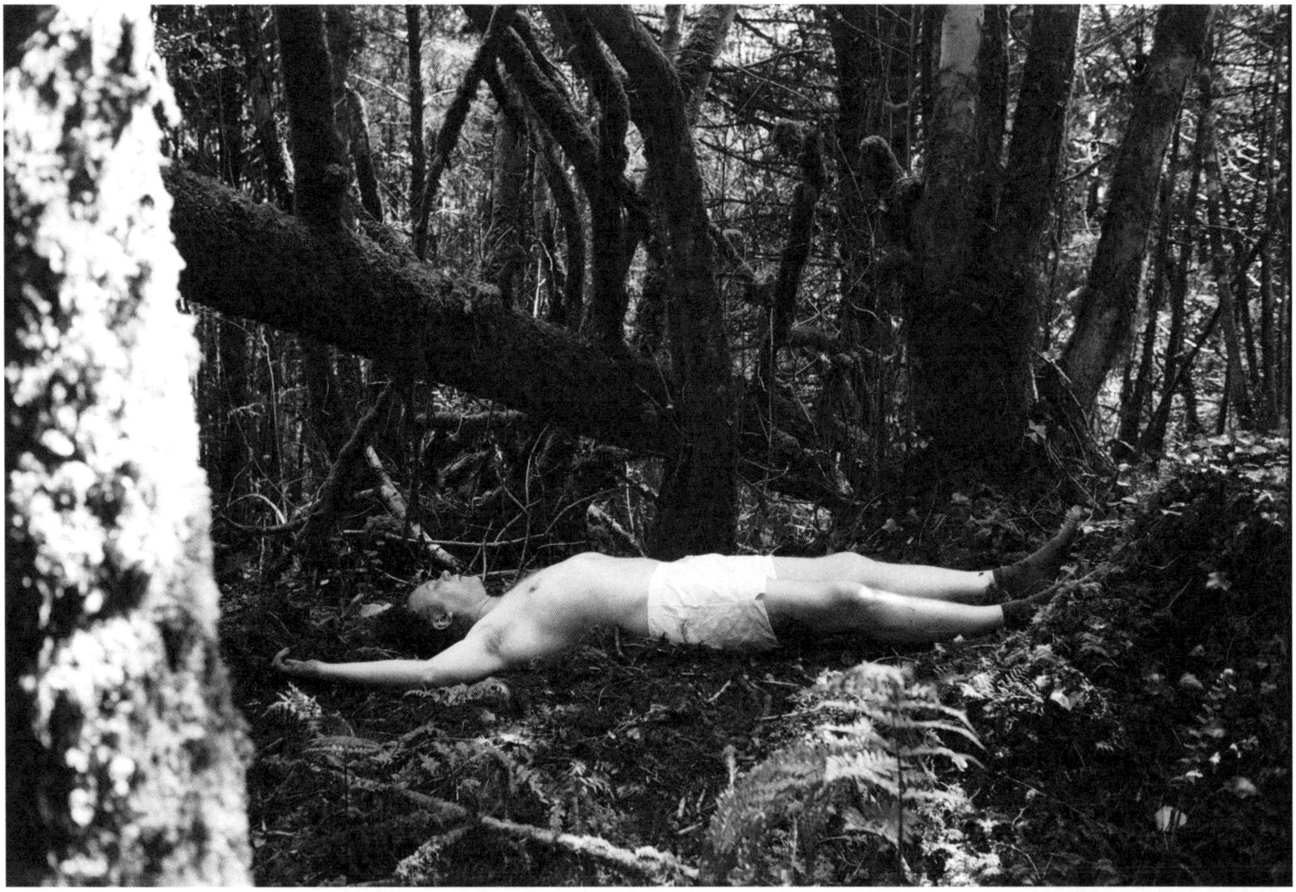

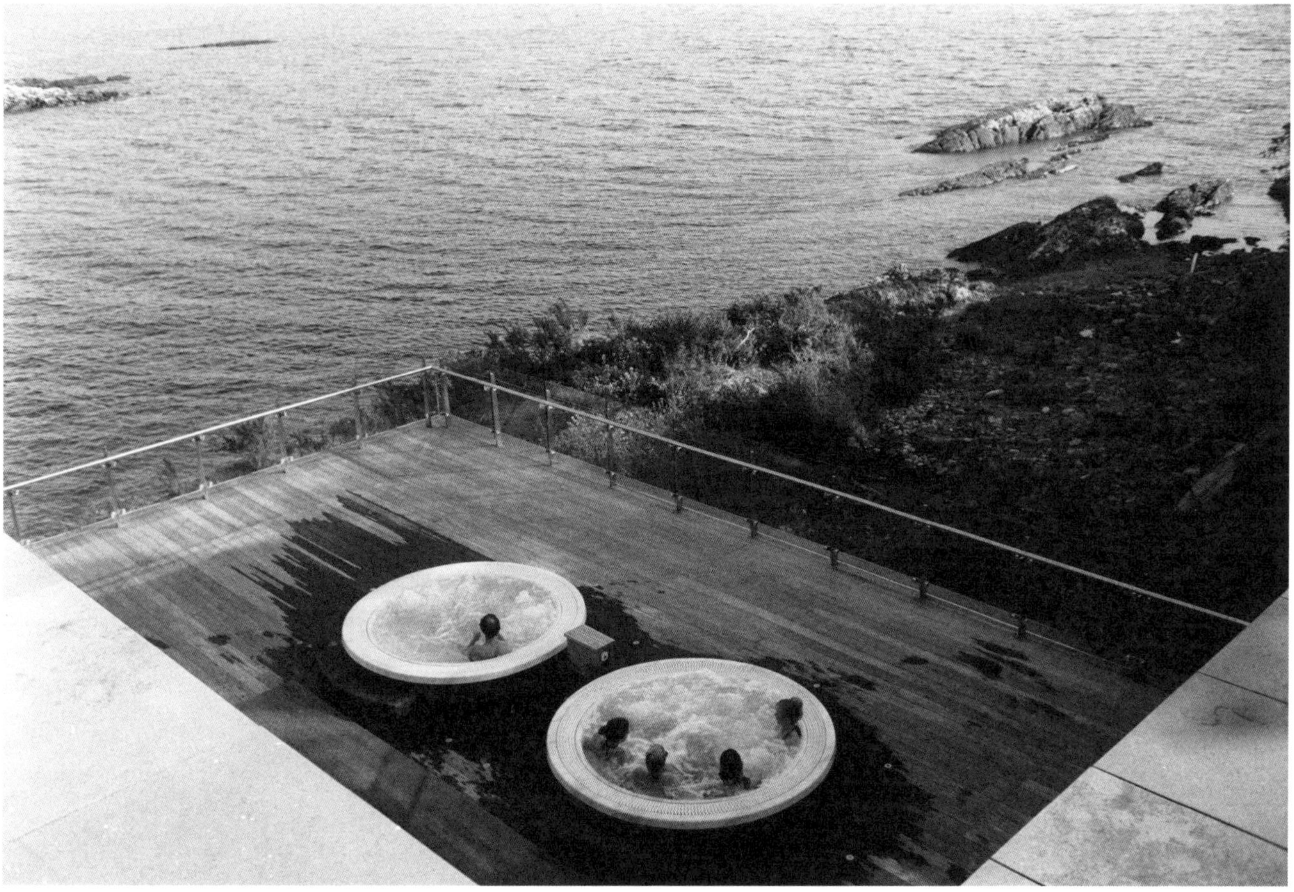

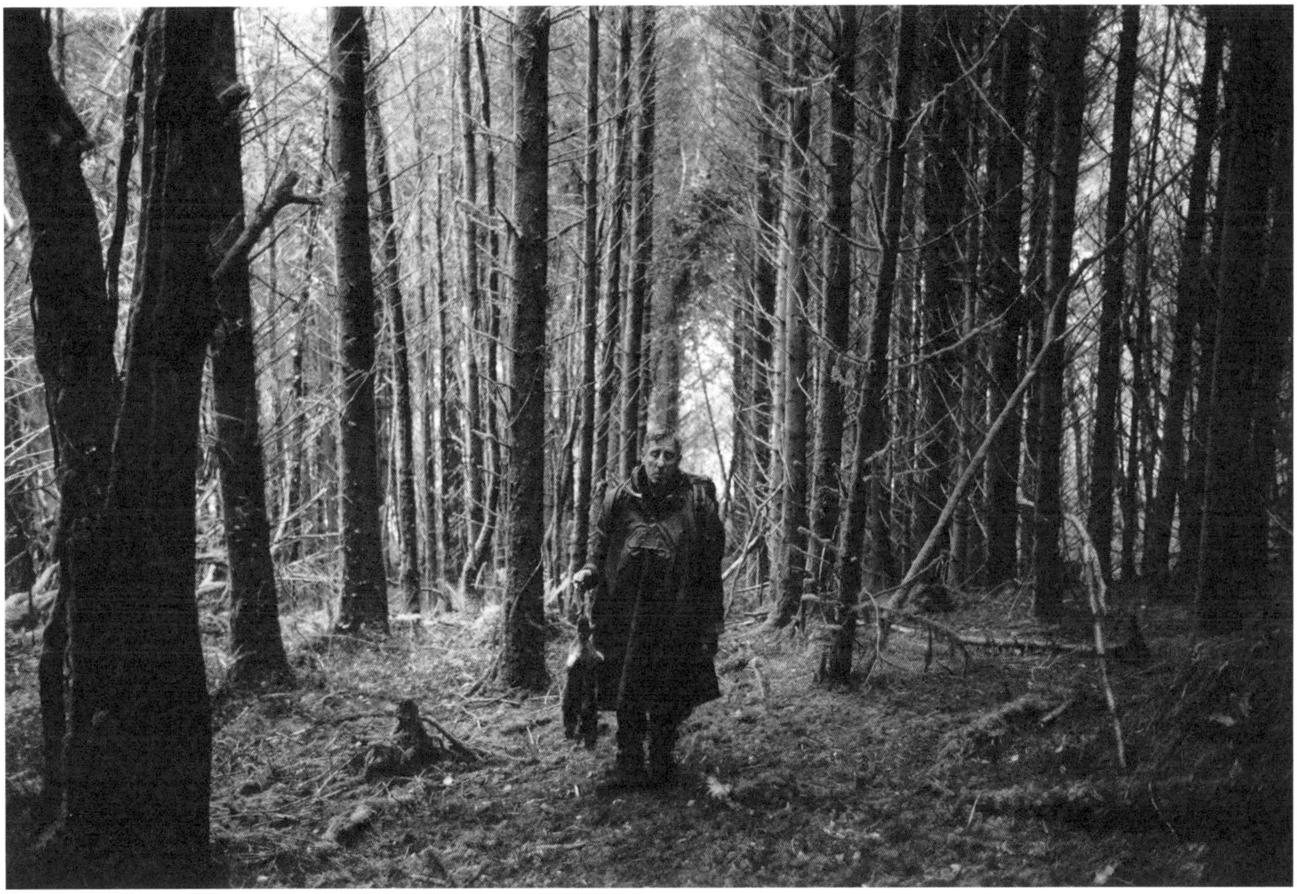

"THE LOBSTER"

DIRECTED BY
YORGOS LANTHIMOS

WRITTEN BY
YORGOS LANTHIMOS & EFTHIMIS FILIPPOU

Film4, Bord Scannán Na Héireann/ The Irish Film Board, Eurimages, The Netherlands Film Fund, Greek Film Centre And BFI
PRESENT

an Element Pictures, Scarlet Films, Faliro House, Haut et Court and Lemming Film
CO-PRODUCTION

WITH THE PARTICIPATION OF
CANAL+
and CINE+

PRODUCED BY
Ed Guiney
Lee Magiday
Ceci Dempsey
Yorgos Lanthimos

CO-PRODUCERS
Christos V. Konstantakopoulos
Leontine Petit
Carole Scotta
Joost de Vries
Derk-Jan Warrink

LINE PRODUCER
Cáit Collins

PRODUCTION DESIGNER
Jacqueline Abrahams

HAIR DESIGNER
Eileen Buggy

IN ASSOCIATION WITH
Protagonist Pictures

IN ASSOCIATION WITH
Limp

WITH THE PARTICIPATION OF
Aide aux Cinémas du Monde, Centre National du Cinéma et de l'Image Animée, Ministère des Affaires Étrangères et du éveloppement International, Institut Français

EXECUTIVE PRODUCERS
Andrew Lowe
Tessa Ross
Sam Lavender

DIRECTOR OF PHOTOGRAPHY
Thimios Bakatakis

EDITED BY
Yorgos Mavropsaridis

CASTING DIRECTOR
Jina Jay

SOUND DESIGNER
Johnnie Burn

COSTUME DESIGNER
Sarah Blenkinsop

MAKE-UP DESIGNER
Sharon Doyle

```
Casting Director.......................................JINA JAY
Line Producer......................................CÁIT COLLINS
Sound Designer....................................JOHNNIE BURN
Production Designer........................JACQUELINE ABRAHAMS
Costume Designer...............................SARAH BLENKINSOP
Hair Designer....................................EILEEN BUGGY
Make-up Designer.................................SHARON DOYLE
```

CAST (IN ALPHABETICAL ORDER)

```
Donkey Shooter...........................JACQUELINE ABRAHAMS
Doctor.................................ROGER ASHTON-GRIFFITHS
Nosebleed Woman.................................JESSICA BARDEN
Hotel Manager.....................................OLIVIA COLMAN
```

70 Year Old Waiter	ANTHONY DOUGALL
Guard Waiter	SEAN DUGGAN
David	COLIN FARRELL
Loner Leader's Father	ROLAND FERRANDI
Bald Man	JAMES FINNEGAN
Restaurant Waiter	ROBERT HEANEY
David's Wife	ROSANNA HOULT
Bob the Dog	JARO and RYAC
Biscuit Woman	ASHLEY JENSEN
Police Officer 1	KATHY KELLY
The Maid	ARIANE LABED
Trainer Waiter (Shooting Range)	EWEN MACINTOSH
Campari Man	PATRICK MALONE
Arrested Town Woman	SANDRA MASON
Police Officer 2	KEVIN MCCORMACK
Bandaged Loner	ISHMAEL MOALOSI
30 Year Old Waiter	ANTHONY MORIARTY
Hotel Manager's Partner	GARRY MOUNTAINE
Guest Room 104	JUDI KING MURPHY
New Daughter	LAOISE MURPHY
Loner Leader's Mother	IMELDA NAGLE RYAN
Hotel Receptionist	NANCY ONU
Trapped Loner	MATTHEW O'BRIEN
Nosebleed Woman's Best Friend	EMMA O'SHEA
Heartless Woman	ANGELIKI PAPOULIA
Lisping Man	JOHN C. REILLY
Loner Leader	LÉA SEYDOUX
Loner Swimmer	MICHAEL SMILEY
Coach Driver Waiter	CHRIS THREADER
Short Sighted Woman	RACHEL WEISZ
Limping Man	BEN WHISHAW

1st Assistant Director	OWEN MAGEE
2nd Assistant Director	LISA KELLY

Post Production Supervisor	VERITY WISLOCKI

Music Supervisor	AMY ASHWORTH

First Assistant Editors	EOIN MCGUIRK
	CONOR MACKEY

3rd Assistant Director	MIKE HAYES
Extras Coordinator	SARAH BETH MOYLAN
Trainee Assistant Directors	STEPHEN RIGNEY
	NIAMH BLANCHE
	ROISIN EL SHERIFF
Production Coordinator	SUSAN MCDAID
Assistant Production Coordinator	PIPPA ROBERTSON
Production Assistant	RUTH POWER
Production Trainee	MARGARET GIBBONS
Production Accountant	REBECCA DALY
Assistant Accountant	JAMES CULLEN

Sound Recordist	MERVYN MOORE
Boom Operator	ROBERT JOHNSTON

```
Sound Trainee..............................................LUKE MCGINLEY


Focus Puller...............................................SHANE DEASY
Clapper Loader.............................................DAVID DOHERTY
DIT........................................................AISLINN MCDONALD
Key Grip...................................................OISÍN KELLY
Camera Trainee.............................................CIARÁN MAGINN
Script Supervisor..........................................DAVE MORAN


Location Manager...........................................EOIN HOLOHAN
Script Supervisor..........................................AYLA O'NEILL
Additional Location Assistant..............................EVELYN O'NEILL
Additional Location Trainees...............................MICHAEL FARRELL
...........................................................EIMEAR O'GRADY
...........................................................JASON O'MAHONY


Property Buyer.............................................KEAVY LALOR
Assistant Art Director.....................................JESSICA TIMLIN
Art Department Trainee.....................................CLARE HYNES
Property Master............................................JIM WALSH
Dressing Props.............................................MARK KELLY
...........................................................MICHAEL FITZPATRICK
Standby Props..............................................DAVE KAVANAGH
Prop Trainee...............................................JAMES DUNNE


Wardrobe Supervisor........................................CASSANDRA STEYN-TAYLOR
Key Set Wardrobe...........................................ROSE LOVE
Costume Assistants.........................................BELLE PHIPPS
...........................................................FRANCESCA DVORAK
Costume Trainee............................................ZUZANA ZILKOVA
...........................................................CAROLINE HARRINGTON
Additional Wardrobe........................................JEN COPELAND
...........................................................RICHELLE CORCORAN
Hairdresser................................................ANNA GRONËRUS
Make-up Artist.............................................LUCY BROWNE
Additional Make-up Trainee.................................ZOE GIBNEY
Additional Hair Trainee....................................ALISON CAHILL


Stunt Coordinator..........................................GIEDRIUS 'GEE' NAGYS
Stunt Performers...........................................EMMA CONDREN
...........................................................AOIFE BYRNE


Colin Farrell Management...................................ILENE FELDMAN
...........................................................CLAUDINE FARRELL


Assistant to Rachel Weisz..................................SUSIE TALBOT


Senior Casting Assistant...................................JESSIE FROST
Junior Casting Assistant...................................OLIVIA BRITTAIN


Casting Director Ireland...................................LOUISE KIELY
Casting Associates Ireland.................................KAREN SCULLY
...........................................................THYRZA GING
Casting Assistant Ireland..................................EVA JANE GAFFNEY
```

```
Extras Casting..........................................MOVIEEXTRAS.IE


Gaffer...................................................BARRY CONROY
Best Boy.................................................PAUL MCNULTY
Additional Electricians....................................MARC COLE
..........................................................IAN KEARNEY


Standby Rigger............................................RICHIE LANG
Standby Stagehand.........................................PAUL O'NEILL


Animal Handlers.....................................COPSEWOOD AVIARIES
...........................................................EDDIE DREW
...........................................................MICK BRADY
.........................................................REBECCA DREW
Bob the Dog's Handler.....................................JULIE HOLMS


Stills Photographer.....................................DESPINA SPYROU
Stills Approval Services.................................FILM SOLUTIONS
............................................................NICK BULL
Unit Publicity..............................................PREMIER
......................................................JONATHAN RUTTER
.........................................................EMMA ROBINSON
EPK Director........................................VINCENT GALLAGHER


Transport Captain......................................MICHAEL PHELAN
Unit Driver................................................KEN QUINN
Additional Transport...............................KERRY EXPERIENCE TOURS
.............................................GERRIT AND ESTER NORDKAMP
Minibus..............................................KERRY COACHES
Camera Truck Driver..............................MICHAEL FARRELL JNR
Facilities Driver...............................JOHN NEE "SQUIRE"
Additional Runaround Vehicles....................BRIAN THOMPSON
.........................................................JASON CLARKE


Armourer..............................................JOHN MCKENNA
Marine Coordinator....................................LIAM O'SHEA
Marine Assistance................IRISH NATIONAL SAILING SCHOOL
......................................................ALISTAIR RUMBALL
Yachts Supplied by................................SOVEREIGN SAILING


Greek Script Translator.........................KYRIACOS KARSERAS
French Script Translators..............JOHN AND ISABELLE MILLER


Trainee Editor....................................ROBERT MCCLELLAND
Additional Post Production Supervisor..........THERESE CALDWELL
Post Production Assistant....................CHARLOTTE LLEWELYN


               DIGITAL INTERMEDIATE BY
                 Storm Post Production

Colourist..............................................TONY FORD
Digital Intermediate Producer........................JACK KUIPER
Online Editor....................................MARTIJN VAN HOUTEN
```

```
Facility Manager..................................................SWAEN NOUWEN


                        VISUAL EFFECTS BY
                              BUF

Visual Effects Supervisor........................OLIVIER CAUWET
On Set Supervisor..............................CHRISTOPHE DUPUIS
Head of Production...................................COLINE SIX
Visual Effects Producer.......................KRISTINA PRILUKOVA
Graphic Artists..................................JONATHAN BONTE
................................................MARTIN CLAUDE
..............................................JOCELYN DEFURNE
..................................................MARION ELOY
..............................................ELEONORE LAISNEY
................................................ANTOINE LHOIR
...............................................ANDRÉ MONTEIRO
..................................................MAXIME NEKO
................................................MATTHIEU PETIT
...............................................DOMINIQUE VIDAL

            ALL BUF CG IMAGES DEVELOPED AND PRODUCED ENTIRELY
                       ON BUF PROPRIETARY SOFTWARE



                     ADDITIONAL VISUAL EFFECTS BY
                        STORM POST PRODUCTION

Digital Compositors..........................DAVID VAN HEESWIJK
..................................................LUUK MEIJER
........................................MARTIN NECAS-NIESSNER
................................................TIMO AALDRIKS



                   SOUND BY WAVE STUDIOS AMSTERDAM

Supervising Sound Editor/Additional Re-recording Mixer..........
..................................................JOHNNIE BURN
Lead Re-recording Mixer/Dialogue Editor.......DANNY VAN SPREUWEL
Sound Effects Editor...........................SIMON CARROLL
Additional Sound Editors.............................JOE MOUNT
..............................................RANDELL MCDONALD
Music Editors.......................MAVROPSARIDIS/BURN/CARROLL
Foley Editor.....................................ERIK GRIEKSPOOR
Foley Artist................................RONNIE VAN DER VEER
Sound Mix Technician.............................ASHLEY SMITH
Additional Music Supervision.......................NICK PAYNE
           SOUND RE-RECORDED AT WARNIERPOSTA, AMSTERDAM



Graphic Design...............................VASILIS MARMATAKIS



                        FOR ELEMENT PICTURES

Head of Business Affairs............................MARK BYRNE
Production Executive ..........................PAULA HEFFERNAN
Head of Development................................EMMA NORTON
Business Affairs Executive.......................FIONA MCCONNELL
Finance Executives..............................DARRAGH NOONAN
..................................................LEONIE QUINN
PA to Company Directors..................CHELSEA MORGAN HOFFMAN
```

Office Manager	VICTORIA OWENS
Production Assistant	EMER O'SHEA
Development/ Production Intern	ALEXANDRA BLUE

FOR SCARLET FILMS

Head of Development	HONOR BORWICK
Head of Creative Affairs	SUE BIRBECK

FOR FALIRO HOUSE

Production Executive	KOSTAS KEFALAS
Legal Counsel	MICHAEL E. TZARTZOURAS
Accountant	CHRYSANTHI FERLE

FOR LEMMING FILM

Project Managers	JURI KEUTER
	RUTH HEIDA
Head of Finance	ELSEMIJN TEULINGS
Assistant Producer	MILAN UEFFING
Production Accountant	HARMEN KREULEN

Executive Producer for Bord Scannán na hÉireann/the Irish Film Board	EMER O'SHEA

FOR BORD SCANNÁN NA HÉIREANN/ THE IRISH FILM BOARD

Chief Executive	JAMES HICKEY
Head of Business Affairs	TERESA MCGRANE
Business and Legal Affairs Coordinator	AILEEN MCCAULEY

FOR FILM4

Development Editor	POLLY STOKES
Head of Editorial	ROSE GARNETT
Senior Legal & Business Affairs Executive	DIMITRA TSINGOU
Production Finance Manager	GERARDINE O'FLYNN
Head of Commercial and Brand Strategy	SUE BRUCE-SMITH

FOR BFI

Director of Lottery Film Fund	BEN ROBERTS
Head of International	ISABEL DAVIS
Development Executive	DAVID SEGAL HAMILTON
Head of Production	FIONA MORHAM
Production Finance	AMANDA PYNE
Business Affairs Manager	BEN WILKINSON

FOR HAUT ET COURT

Associate Producers	SIMON ARNAL
	CAROLINE BENJO
Line Producer	JULIE BILLY

```
Head of Financing and Administration............OLIVIER PASQUIER
Accountant......................................JULIEN BERTHEUIL
Secretary.....................................SABRIA YAHIA-CHERIF


                    FOR HAUT ET COURT DISTRIBUTION

Head of Distribution.............................LAURENCE PETIT
Acquisition - Co-Productions.....................LAURE CAILLOL
Marketing Manager..............................MARION THARAUD
New Media Manager..............................MARTIN GRANGER
Sales Managers...................................MARTIN BIDOU
..............................................CHRISTELLE OSCAR
Servicing Manager............................NICOLAS VOILLARD
Accountant.....................................STÉPHANIE LORIOT


                    FOR PROTAGONIST PICTURES

Chief Executive Officer..........................MIKE GOODRIDGE
Head of Legal and Business Affairs...............SIMON OSBORN
Head of Sales....................................VANESSA SAAL
Head of Marketing.............................BRIDGET PEDGRIFT
Head of Worldwide Acquisitions....................DAVE BISHOP
Delivery Manager...............................HASHIM ALSARAF


                         FOR EURIMAGES

Project Managers..............................ALESSIA SONAGLIONI
............................................SUSAN NEWMAN-BAUDAIS


Medical Support........................................ESTI
Paramedic...................................TREVOR HORNIBROOK
Security...........................GREENSHIELDS SECURITY
Location Catering....................................LOCATOR
Facilities...............................MOVIES ON THE MOVE
Genie Boom...............................MB ACCESS SOLUTIONS
Additional Edit Equipment Rental....................TYRELL LTD
.............................................RAZOR CUT POST
Retail Banking........................................AIB
Clearances.....................................PAULA DALY
Title Report and Opinion............LAW OFFICES OF DENNIS ANGEL
Copyright Report..............................THOMSON COMPUMARK


Post Production Script by........................SAPEX SCRIPTS
Access Services by.......................................DELUXE


Completion Guarantor............................FILM FINANCES
................................................NEIL CALDER
................................................RUTH HODGSON
Collection Agent serviced by...................FREEWAY CAM B.V.


Production Legal Services.................PHILIP LEE SOLICITORS
...............................................JONATHAN KELLY
.................................................CIAN MCELHONE
```

```
Production Finance..........................................COFILOISIRS
............................................................DOMINIQUE MALET
......................................................JEAN BAPTISTE SOUCHIER
S481 Finance.......................CROWE HORWATH BASTOW CHARLETON
.................................................................JOHN GLEESON
..............................................................ROISIN HENEHAN
.............................................................NAOISE COSGROVE


Insurance provided by...................................TRAVELERS LTD
...........................................c/o MEDIA INSURANCE BROKERS LTD
..............................................................JOHN O'SULLIVAN


Auditor..................................................CROWE HORWATH


Camera and Grip Equipment......................PANAVISION IRELAND
Lighting Equipment......................................CINE ELECTRIC


Props supplied by...........................HISTORIC INTERIORS
...........................................................................AM PM
Clothing manufactured by.......................FASHION HOTHOUSE
Cosmetics supplied by...........................MAC COSMETICS
Colin Farrell's Eyewear supplied by...'OPTICA' DONAL MCNALLY JNR
Travel Agent..................................................FLAIR TRAVEL
Couriers..................................................AERFAST COURIERS
..........................................................CYCLONE COURIERS
```

FILMED ON LOCATION AT PARKNASILLA HOTEL AND RESORT
AND DOMORE WOODS, COILLTE TEORANTA

DON QUIXOTE: VARIATION I AND II
Composed by Richard Strauss
Published by C. F. Peters Leipzig
Licensed by Peters Edition Ltd, London
All rights reserved.
International copyright secured.
Performed by Staatskapelle Dresden,
conducted by Fabio Luisi
Courtesy of Sony Music Germany GmbH

STRING QUARTET NO. 8 IN C MINOR,
OP. 110; 4. LARGO
Composed by Dmitri Shostakovich
Permission of Boosey & Hawkes,
an Imagem Company
Performed by Emerson String Quartet
Courtesy of Deutsche Grammophon
Under licence from Universal Music
Operations Ltd

3 PIECES FOR STRING QUARTET NO. 3
Composed by Igor Stravinsky
Permission of Boosey & Hawkes,
an Imagem Company
Performed by Goldner String Quartet
Courtesy of Naxos Rights US Inc.

STRING QUARTET NO. 1 IN D, OP. 25:
ANDANTE SOSTENUTO
Composed by Benjamin Britten
Permission of Boosey & Hawkes,
an Imagem Company
Performed by the Takács Quartet
Courtesy of Hyperion Records
Ltd, London

STRING QUARTET IN F MAJOR, OP. 18, NO.
1; II ADAGIO AFFETUOSO ED APPASIONATO
Composed By Ludwig Van Beethoven
Performed By Julliard String Quartet
Courtesy Of Sony Music
Entertainment Inc.

APO MESA PETHAMENOS
Music and Lyrics by Attik
Performed by Danae
Courtesy of Cobalt Music

WHERE THE WILD ROSES GROW
Written by Nick Cave
Performed by Colin Farrell
Published by Mute Song Ltd
Courtesy of Mute Records Ltd.
A BMG Company

SOMETHING'S GOTTEN HOLD OF MY HEART
Written by Cook/Greenaway
Published by Universal/
Dick James Music Ltd
Performed by Olivia Colman and
Garry Mountaine
Performance arrangement by Cian Boylan

STRING QUARTET NO. 2: I MODERATO
Composed by Alfred Schnittke
Permission of Boosey & Hawkes,
an Imagem Company
Performed by The Tale Quartet
With kind permission of
BIS Record, Sweden

BAROQUE DANCE
Performed by Roland Ferrandi and
Imelda Nagle Ryan
Written by Gaspar Sanz
Arranged as guitar duet by
Roland Ferrandi

HANDBAG
Written and Performed by Johnnie Burn
Published by Tonic Music Ltd

BLEEP DISCO
Written and Performed by Johnnie Burn
Published by Tonic Music Ltd

HOG SHUFFLE
Written and Performed by Johnnie Burn
Published by Tonic Music Ltd

WHERE THE WILD ROSES GROW
Written by Nick Cave
Performed by Nick Cave & The Bad
Seeds and Kylie Minogue
Published by Mute Song Ltd
Courtesy of Mute Records Ltd.
A BMG Company

JEUX INTERDIT (ANON.)
Performed by Roland Ferrandi
and Imelda Nagle Ryan
Arranged as guitar duet by
Roland Ferrandi

TI EIN AFTO POU TO LENE AGAPI
Performed by Tonis Maroudas
and Sophia Loren
Composer Morakis / Takis Panagiotis
Lyrics by Fermanoglou / Gianis Ioannis
Courtesy of AEPI (the Hellenic
Society for the protection
of IntellectualProperty S.A.)
Courtesy of Twentieth Century
Fox Film Corporation

LONER DUB
Written and Performed by Johnnie Burn
Published by Tonic Music Ltd

QUINTET FOR PIANO AND STRINGS:
IN TEMPO DI VALSE
Composed by Alfred Schnittke
Published by C. F. Peters Ltd &
Co. KG, Leipzig
Licensed by Peters Edition Ltd, London
All rights reserved.
International copyright secured.
Performed by Borodin Quartet
Courtesy of Warner Music UK Ltd

MILLION $ FEAT. MILLA M
Composed by Benjamin John Tomlin (PRS)

SPECIAL THANKS TO
ESTATE OF ATTIK, JAY BAKER, MATTHEW BATES, JEREMY BAXTER,
BERO BEYER, DOREEN BOONEKAMP, JASON CLARKE, PEG DONEGAN,
JANE EPSTEIN, JAMES FARRELL, MARY FITZGERALD, SAM FOX,
CHRISTIAN HODDELL, OLIVIA HOMAN, SHARON JACKSON,
KERRY CO. COUNCIL, DAVID KOPPLE, ARIANE LABED, DIXIE LINDER,
SOPHIA LOREN, JOEL LUBIN, ESTATE OF TONIS MAROUDAS,
GRAEME MASON, CONOR MCCAUGHAN, ALEX MEBED,
PARKNASILLA HOTEL AND RESORT AND THE COMMUNITY OF SNEEM,
CO. KERRY, IRELAND, FRANK PEIJNENBURG, SARA PURO,
HYLDA QUEALLY, IRINA SHOSTAKOVICH, MAXIM AND
GALINA SHOSTAKOVICH, THE TEAM AT ELEMENT PICTURES DISTRIBUTION

THANKS TO
MAGALIE ARMAND, ARGIRO CHIOTI, DERMOT CLEARY,
NATHALIE COSTE CERDAN, TONY DALY, DAVIDOFF, SAMANTHA DINNING,
IZZI DUNN, MOSELLE FOLEY, GERBOLA CIRCUS, ALEXIS GRIVAS,
LAURENT HASSID, DIMITRA KAKOULIDI, EVA KAKOULIDOU, EMMA KEAVENEY,
KATE KENNELLY, PAT DAWSON - KILLARNEY NATIONAL PARK,
EDWARD LAWRENSON, JAMES LYONS, NICKY MACMANUS, CATHERINE MAGEE,
MARIE MCDONNELL, CHRISTINE MERGOUPI, MNP DESIGN STUDIO,
EAMON MURPHY, JIM O'BRIEN, ROBERTO OLLA, RUTH O'SULLIVAN,
INDIA OSBORNE, STELLA PAGE, ANTONIA PAGULATOS,
PANAGIOTIS PANTELATOS, KATERINA PAPANAGIOTOU, IOANNA PAPARA,
THANOS PAPASTERGIOU, HANNAH PEEL, ALEXIS PERRIN, SIMONS RODENTS,
KOTONO SATO, EMMA SCOTT, MELITA SKAMNAKI, MARIOS SCHWAB,
YIOTA SKOUVARA, SNEEM HOTEL, IRINI SOUGANIDOU, SPOOKY,
KAMIEL VAN DER STER, NATHALIE STREIFF, CHRISTOS VOUDOURIS,
KRISTINA ZIMMERMANN

AN IRISH – UK – GREEK – FRENCH - DUTCH CO-PRODUCTION
UNDER THE EUROPEAN CONVENTION ON CINEMATOGRAPHIC CO-PRODUCTION

FILMED ON LOCATION IN IRELAND. PRODUCED WITH THE SUPPORT
OF INVESTMENT INCENTIVES FOR THE IRISH FILM INDUSTRY PROVIDED
BY THE GOVERNMENT OF IRELAND

© ELEMENT PICTURES / SCARLET FILMS /
FALIRO HOUSE PRODUCTIONS SA / HAUT ET COURT /
LEMMING FILM/ THE BRITISH FILM INSTITUTE /
CHANNEL FOUR TELEVISION CORPORATION 2015

ALL RIGHTS RESERVED

THE CHARACTERS, INCIDENTS AND EVENTS PORTRAYED ARE FICTITIOUS
AND ANY SIMILARITY TO THE NAME, CHARACTER OR HISTORY OF ANY
PERSON LIVING OR DEAD IS PURELY COINCIDENTAL AND UNINTENTIONAL.

THIS MOTION PICTURE IS PROTECTED UNDER THE LAWS OF THE REPUBLIC
OF IRELAND AND OTHER COUNTRIES. ANY UNAUTHORIZED EXHIBITION,
DISTRIBUTION OR REPRODUCTION OF THIS MOTION PICTURE OR ANY PART
THEREOF (INCLUDING SOUNDTRACK) MAY RESULT IN SEVERE CIVIL AND
CRIMINAL PENALTIES.

PUBLISHER
A24 Films LLC
New York, NY
a24films.com

CREATIVE DIRECTION
Zoe Beyer

HEAD OF PUBLISHING
Perrin Drumm

EDITORS
Mark Lotto
Margaret Rhodes

COPY EDITOR
Todd Albright

COLORIST
David Herr

SPECIAL THANKS
Kyra Goldstein

ART DIRECTION AND DESIGN
Actual Source
50 E 500 N #103
Provo, UT
actualsource.work

TYPOGRAPHY
Ivory Mono Light
Ivory Mono Medium
Ivory Bold
Ivory Regular
 (Aurèle Sack)
Parma Normal
Parma Normal Italic
 (Dinamo)

TIP-IN
GardaGloss 135 g

PAPER
Munken Polar Rough 100 g
GardaGloss 150 g

PRINTER
Conti Tipocolor
Via Guido Guinizelli, 20
50041 Calenzano FI, Italy

©2022 the authors, editors, and owners of all respective content.

All rights reserved; no part of this publication may be reproduced, stored in a retrieval system, or transmitted in any form or by any means, electronic, mechanical, photocopying, recording, or otherwise, without prior written consent of the publisher.

ISBN 978-1-7359117-1-7

A24